KINGDOM
MANAGEMENT *for*
ANOINTED
PROSPERITY

By Dr. Alan Pateman

1. The Reality of a Warrior

2. Healing and Deliverance, A Present Reality

3. Control, A Powerful Force

4. His Life is in the Blood

5. Sexual Madness, In a Sexually Confused World (co-authored with Jennifer Pateman)

6. Apostles, Can the Church Survive Without Them?

7. Prayer, Ingredients for Successful Intercession, Part One

8. Prayer, Touching the Heart of God, Part Two

9. The Early Years, Anointed Generals Past and Present, Part One of Four

10. Revival Fires, Anointed Generals Past and Present, Part Two of Four

11. Why War, A Biblical Approach to the Armour of God and Spiritual Warfare

12. Forgiveness, the Key to Revival

13. His Faith, Positions us for Possession

14. Seduction & Control: Infiltrating Society and the Church

15. Kingdom Management for Anointed Prosperity

16. TONGUES, our Supernatural Prayer Language

17. Seven Pillars for Life and Kingdom Prosperity

18. WINNING by Mastering your Mind

19. Laying Foundations

20. Apostles and the Local Church

21. Preparations for Ministry

22. Developments and Provision

23. The Age of Apostolic Apostleship

24. *Media, Spiritual Gateway (co-authored with Jennifer Pateman)*

25. *Israel, the Question of Ownership*

26. *Earnestly Contending for the State of Israel*

27. *The Temple, Antichrist and the New World Order*

28. *The Antichrist, Rapture and the Battle of Armageddon*

29. *Israel, the Church and the End Times*

30. *Introduction to all things APMI*

31. *Student's Handbook, Study Guide Volume 2*

32. *Empowered to Overcome*

33. *Equipped for Spiritual Warfare*

34. *Appropriations of African Territory*

35. *Coronavirus, World War III*

36. *China, Covid-19 and World Domination*

BY DR. JENNIFER PATEMAN

1. *Sexual Madness, In a Sexually Confused World (co-authored with Alan Pateman)*

2. *Millennial Myopia, From a Biblical Perspective*

3. *Media, Spiritual Gateway (co-authored with Alan Pateman)*

AVAILABLE FROM APMI PUBLICATIONS, AMAZON.COM AND OTHER RETAIL OUTLETS

KINGDOM
MANAGEMENT
for
ANOINTED
PROSPERITY

DR. ALAN PATEMAN

BOOK TITLE:
Kingdom Management for Anointed Prosperity

WRITTEN BY Dr. ALAN PATEMAN
ISBN: 978-1-909132-34-4
eBook ISBN: 978-1-909132-51-1

Published By:
APMI Publications
In Partnership with Truth for the Journey Books **15**
Email: publications@alanpateman.com
www.AlanPatemanMinistries.com

Acknowledgements:
Author/Design/Senior Editor/Publisher: Apostle Dr. Alan Pateman
Editing/Proofreading/Research: Dr. Jennifer Pateman
Computer Administration/Office Manager: Dr. Dorothea Struhlik
Cover Image Credit: © Lukas Gojda www.fotolia.com

❖

Dedication

With great admiration and respect I dedicate this book to all my colleagues, pastors, leaders and friends, with whom I have the greatest pleasure of working with. Especially to my Executive Trustees, for all their valuable support:

- **Dr. Jennifer Pateman,** Vice President of Alan Pateman Ministries Int., Co-Host of Connecting for Excellence Int. Network, and Editorial Consultant of LifeStyle Int. Christian University
- **Dr. Henry O. Ogbebor,** District Pastor of Christ Apostolic Church of God Mission Int. Inc. (CACGM worldwide) Italy
- **Dr. Benjamin A. Asare,** President of World Missions Ministries and Senior Pastor of Followers of Christ Int. Church Novara, Italy
- **Dr. Dorothea Struhlik,** Executive Dean of LifeStyle Int. Christian University

May God truly increase your lives and I pray that the anointing of His Prosperity rests on you all.

❖

Table of Contents

Introduction..11

Chapter 1   Kingdom Management..............................15

Chapter 2   So What's Your Crisis?..........................21

Chapter 3   Managing Appetites.............................29

Chapter 4   Our Key to Success............................35

Chapter 5   Don't Jump Ship!..............................41

Chapter 6   God's Financial Plan..........................49

Chapter 7   Underground Cash Economy......................63

Chapter 8   Alms, A Vital Decision........................73

Chapter 9   Appropriating God's Word......................83

Chapter 10   Get in Line for a Spiritual Harvest!..........89

Chapter 11   Victims or Investors?................................95

Chapter 12   Break Out Prosperity................................101

Chapter 13   The Spirit of Increase................................107

Chapter 14   True Partnership A Faith Venture................113

❖

Introduction

I wrote this book, because I became restless with all the crisis I was seeing in the lives of so many around the world. I travel extensively due to working internationally within the Body of Christ and at the very beginning of 2015, God spoke clearly and gave me what I believe to be a prophetic word for this season: **management.**

The more I began pondering, studying, praying over this word "management" (and seeking interpretation from the Holy Spirit), revelation began to flow! I had the realisation that much of the Body of Christ - desperately require a greater understanding of what it means to manage their affairs properly. Life has to be managed and managed well, if we are to be successful.

This book is not about money, although that does come into it, because in life we need money, yet "Kingdom

Management for Anointed Prosperity" is so much more than that. And I pray that as you read on, God by His Spirit will reveal new ways in which you can start managing your personal affairs better: your life, your friends, your job, your health, your wealth, your family - marriage, children - your studies, your ministry or church, your business, your career; your skills and talents.

There are so many more life categories, (to add to the few that I've just mentioned), but it must be said about all of them; if we manage them well; all will be well. If we manage them poorly, all will not be well. "How profoundly deep," you are! Yet we do often miss the simplest aspects of life that make the biggest difference.

So there is more to Kingdom Management for Anointed Prosperity, than just money, silver or gold. When God gives us gifts or talents for instance; they do us no good, unless we possess the wisdom to know how to handle them properly.

Prosperity is more about overall "well-being," in every area of life. Prosperity describes (physical, mental and spiritual) wholeness (peace) not just a robust bank balance! Wholeness is a state of completion; where nothing is missing or broken. It's a condition called peace, where life works and there is reduced dysfunction.

How the world needs to see what Jesus looks like! But who'll be convinced by our dysfunctional lives? How can we take the nations for God, if we can't even mange our dirty dishes, washing the car, keeping a tidy house and taking out the trash; especially if we can't manage a healthy church or raise well-adjusted children at home?

This life is all about management and let's be honest, we will never manage the rest of the world, if we can't manage our own world's first! And it's pointless striving for prosperity, when we aren't competent of managing our everyday affairs. In short - whatever we mis-manage will fail miserably, but whatever we manage well - will succeed!

> *His master replied, "Well done, good and faithful servant! You have been faithful with a few things; I will put you in charge of many things. Come and share your master's happiness!"*
>
> *(Matthew 25: 21)*

Finally sharing his thoughts on crisis management Myles Munroe wrote: "Every single human being is supposed to be a manager... When the Lord God made the earth and filled it up with resources, the very next thing He had to do was to make a manager to take care of it." He went on to say, "Your faith is only as strong as the crisis it survives."

I know that "Kingdom Management for Anointed Prosperity" will provide you with an awesome life-tool, as well as for ministry.

— Dr. Alan Pateman

❖

CHAPTER 1

Kingdom Management

Welcome to anointed prosperity, in this chapter we are looking at the subject of **Kingdom Management.** I believe it's a crucial concept that each of us need to grasp. **Without sound management in our lives, everything is given to chaos, of which God is not the author,** "For God is not the author of confusion, but of **peace**... " (1 Corinthians 14:33 KJV)

The word *"peace,"* which is *"shalom"* in Hebrew and *"eirene"* in Greek means: *completeness, health, soundness, welfare, perfect (nothing missing or broken); security, safety, prosperity (see Strong's H7965; G1515).*

So in a nutshell, peace in our lives is a result of good management.

The Management of the Holy Spirit

The Holy Spirit gets to work on our chaos the moment we are born again! He will not cohabit with chaos. Therefore if we are to host the presence of God, we must allow Him to work on our lives: "Don't you know that **your body is the temple of the Holy Spirit** who comes from God and dwells inside of you? You do not own yourself. You have been **purchased at a great price**, so use your body to **bring glory to God!**" (1 Corinthians 6:19-20 VOICE)

Quite frankly, chaos does not glorify God! And like you perhaps, I came to God, a-walking-mess! I needed His order in my life. I may have been a willing recipient but that doesn't imply that gaining control over my chaos came easily for me - no way!

It was years (and with much deliverance) before God's order began to reign sovereign in my heart and in my actions. I simply couldn't remain the same. I had to change. We all have to change. We can come as we are and be accepted - but then we must change, in fact it's impossible to stay the same. **The Holy Spirit is God's Agent for Change!**

Now, chaos might be all around us but it must not be in us! So we must yield to the change. Then as each storm comes, we don't mutate or become part of the storm, instead we overcome! Understand something today - you were designed to overcome. Jesus did not eject us. He left us here, to overcome. And that is what we must do. We have an unbeatable Spirit. Winning is in our nature!

He that OVERCOMETH shall inherit ALL THINGS;
and I will be his God, and he shall be my son.

(Revelation 21:7)

Overcoming Crisis

Living here in Italy, one **word** people like to use a lot is **"crisis!"** Italy's not generally known for sound-management especially in the area of politics, (which is burdensomely bureaucratic!) You can get tied up in red tape here, if you don't know how to navigate!

In fact Italians in general don't trust their government and politicians in particular. Another country currently making headlines here in Europe is Greece; due to it's perceived lack of economic management. This of course puts pressure on the Euro and is something that sophisticated Germany [who has, yet again, emerged as the powerhouse of Europe] is not too pleased about!

So let's say that most crisis, especially the economic kind, results from mismanagement, fear, a lack of knowledge and greed. We see this in Matthew chapter 25, where two parables are given to describe what the Kingdom of God will be like.

The first parable was about Ten Virgins and the second about the poor management of money!

*At that time the kingdom of heaven will be like… a man going on a journey, who called his servants and **entrusted his wealth to them**. To one he gave five bags of gold, to another two bags, and to another one bag, **each according to his ability**. Then he went on his journey. The man* *who had received five bags of gold went **at once and put his money to work** and gained five bags more. So also, the one with two bags of gold gained two more. **But the man who had received one bag went off, dug a hole in the ground and hid his master's money.***

*After a long time the master of those servants returned and settled accounts with them. The man who had received five bags of gold brought the other five. "Master," he said, "you entrusted me with five bags of gold. See, I have gained five more." His master replied, **"Well done, good and faithful servant! You have been faithful with a few things; I will put you in charge of many things.** Come and share your master's happiness!"*

*The man with two bags of gold also came. "Master," he said, "you entrusted me with two bags of gold; see, I have gained two more." His master replied, **"Well done, good and faithful servant! You have been faithful with a few things; I will put you in charge of many things.** Come and share your master's happiness!"*

*Then the man who had received one bag of gold came. "Master," he said, "I knew that you are a hard man, harvesting where you have not sown and gathering where you have not scattered seed. **So I was afraid and went out and hid your gold in the ground. See, here is what belongs to you."***

*His master replied, **"You wicked, lazy servant!** So you knew that I harvest where I have not sown and gather where I have not scattered seed? Well then, you should* *have put my money on deposit with the bankers, so that when I returned I would have received it back with interest.*

So take the bag of gold from him and give it to the one who has ten bags. For whoever has will be given more, and they will have an abundance. Whoever does not have, even what they have will be taken from them. And throw that worthless servant outside, into the darkness, where there will be weeping and gnashing of teeth."

(Matthew 25:1; 14-30)

Fear Stops Productivity

The scripture above states that, "The man who had received five bags of gold **went at once and put his money to work** and gained five bags more." His fearless demeanour produced much fruit - and without difficulty.

However the servant who operated out of fear was much less fruitful. In fact his master didn't take too kindly to being falsely accused by this "wicked and lazy servant," who not only accused him of being a "hard man" but of steeling no less! "…harvesting where you have not sown and gathering where you have not scattered seed."

So why did this servant behave so differently to the other servants? The obvious answer is FEAR! "**I was afraid and went out and hid your gold in the ground. See, here is what belongs to you.**" Fear causes us to mismanage what is placed in our charge. When we strive instead of thrive, fear is present. When we become threatened and suspicious - fear is present. When we are non-productive - fear is present.

We must never operate out of fear - it is a totally wrong spirit (see 2 Timothy 1:7). **Fear causes poor judgment and results in poor management.** "Wicked and lazy servants" refuse to take responsibility and prefer taking the safer position of judging, criticising and accusing others, (including God!)

In Christ, we have been called to be **good and faithful servants who are faithful with few things, so that we can be put in charge of many (see Matthew 25:21).**

❖

CHAPTER 2

So What's Your Crisis?

What kind of crisis are you in right now? Perhaps if you trace it back to its source, you'll discover that mismanagement and greed are at its core? Perhaps you've even been the victim of someone else's greed and mismanagement, if not your own?

For example we can see in today's economy, that it's always the poor who suffer the most, from the greed of others. When the big banks got greedy and made their mistakes, they got bailed out and just carried on as usual [the fat cats still received their fat bonuses!] But it's the low-income folks, who are still footing the bill! This bites... especially when the banks play it safe — they don't have to suffer the consequences of their mismanagement and greed - yet everyone else must!

Take Courage Jesus has Overcome the World!

A crisis will make you a victim if you are not careful. It might not have been your fault, but you can control your "coming-out!" In the same context; you might not have chosen the hand you were dealt, but you can choose how you play it!

Here is a short list of some of the complex emotions experienced from a crisis: worry, self pity, depression, dread (fear of loss), misery, discouragement, defeatism, fatalism (especially joblessness), negativity, cynicism, brooding loneliness, grieving, frustration, anxiety, despair and hopelessness, self-hate, humiliation, demoralisation, and **in some cases unresolved trauma.** This can go on to develop abandonment issues, fear of death and obsessive-self-preservation (paranoia).

In spite of all this, any crisis can and *must* be overcome. Jesus did not pull any punches because He openly warned us about the ongoing crisis in this world:

> *...in this godless world you will continue to experience difficulties.*
>
> *(John 16:33 MSG)*

> *...in the world ye shall have dis-ease.*
>
> *(John 16:33 WYC)*

> *...many trials and sorrows.*
>
> *(John 16:33 NLT)*

> *...plagued with times of trouble.*
>
> *(John 16:33 VOICE)*

However if our foundation is the Solid-Rock of Christ (and not sand) we can go through *any* storm: "Trust in the Lord (commit yourself to Him, lean on Him, hope confidently in Him) forever; for the Lord God is an everlasting Rock [the **Rock of Ages**]" (Isaiah 26:4 AMP).

We'll still experience storms - no matter how well insulated we think our lives are - one after the other! The point is learning how to overcome and recover from the storms - not analyse them! In Christ we are over-comers and the book of Revelations gives this mighty assurance: **"HE THAT OVERCOMETH SHALL INHERIT ALL THINGS..."** (Revelations 21:7 KJV)

Christ is our Leverage

If we don't manage ourselves, the crisis will manage us. Then all sorts of negative things can start happening. For example individuals, who aren't coping with life, resort to all manner of coping mechanisms: drug abuse, sexual abuse, physical or verbal and psychology abuse.

On the extreme end of the scale, some people even become psychotic *(severely mentally ill - deranged)*. Yet Jesus said, **"...but be of good cheer [take courage; be confident, certain, undaunted]! For I have overcome the world. [I have deprived it of power to harm you and have conquered it for you]"** (John 16:33 AMP).

In all these things we are more than conquerors through him who loved us. For I am convinced that neither death nor life, neither angels nor demons, neither *the present nor the future, nor any powers, neither height nor depth, nor anything else in all creation, will be able to separate us from the love of God that is in **Christ Jesus our Lord.***

(Romans 8:37-39)

There is no alternative to Christ. Short-lived victories that some people seem to enjoy in this life will not last forever: "Don't bother your head with braggarts or wish you could succeed like the wicked. In no time they'll shrivel like grass clippings and wilt like cut flowers in the sun…" (Psalm 37:1-2 MSG)

Measure Success with Christ not the Culture

*Take your everyday, ordinary life – your sleeping, eating, going-to-work, and walking-around life – and place it before God as an offering. Embracing what God does for you is the best thing you can do for him. **Don't become so well-adjusted to your culture that you fit into it without even thinking.** Instead, fix your attention on God. You'll be changed from the inside out. Readily recognize what he wants from you, and quickly respond to it. **Unlike the culture around you, always dragging you down to its level of immaturity, God brings the best out of you**, develops well-formed maturity in you.*

(Romans 12:1 MSG)

Greed Motivates Mismanagement

This element plays havoc with our ability to manage; greed is so hazardous and menacing.

According to Myles Munroe greed is, "...the mismanagement of resources for personal benefit, coupled with a disregard for the benefit of others. Greed is when you want more than you need at the expense of everybody else" (Munroe 19).

> *You can be sure of this: No one will have a place in the kingdom of Christ and of God who sins sexually, or does evil things, **or is greedy. Anyone who is greedy is serving a false god.***
>
> *(Ephesians 5:5 NCV)*

The definition of greed in the English language according to the Merriam-Webster Dictionary is: *"a selfish and excessive desire for more of something (as money) than is needed."*

The Greek definition for *"greed"* is: *covetousness (G4124). [Covetous basically means: an intense desire for things that you don't currently posses - especially those things that belong to someone else!]*

In Amos 3:3 it says, "Can two walk together, except they be agreed?" (KJV) Greed also has many unholy alliances, such as those named in Mark 7:21-22, "For it is from within, out of a person's heart, that evil thoughts come — sexual immorality, theft, murder, adultery, **greed**, malice, deceit, lewdness, envy, slander, arrogance and folly."

Greed is synonymous with lust and covetousness: "Every man is tempted, when he is drawn away of his own **lust**, and enticed" (James 1:14 KJV). The Wycliffe bible uses the word covet, "Each man is tempted, drawn and stirred of his own

coveting… drawn from reason, and snared, or deceived." The Message bible is different again: "The temptation to give in to evil comes from us and only us. We have no one to blame but the leering, seducing flare-up of our own **lust.**"

Managing our Hearts

Managing our hearts (and mouths) is not just a case of weeding an inner garden full of weeds (wrong thoughts), it's much more than that. "Above all else, **guard** [govern, manage] your heart, for everything you do flows from it" (Proverbs 4:23 [emphasis added]). Greed is a condition of the heart and we must govern our hearts well. Hebrew for *guarding* your heart means: *"to watch over, keep, preserve, guard from dangers, guard with fidelity, keep secret, to be kept close, be blockaded" (Strong's H5341).*

In addition - about the heart - Jeremiah said, "The heart is deceitful **above all things,** and **desperately wicked**…" (17:9 KJV) Without Christ we cannot contend with our own hearts, (high maintenance is an understatement!)

Our hearts have a lot to answer for: "…of the abundance of the heart his mouth speaketh" (Luke 6:45 KJV). It's our words that are the dead-give-away. They reveal the contents of our heart, and it's the unmanaged contents of our hearts that defile us: "The things that come out of your mouth — your curses, your fears, your denunciations — these come from your heart, and it is the stirrings of your heart that can make you unclean" (Matthew 15:18 VOICE).

It takes more than human effort. It takes supernatural management to govern the human heart. "I am the One who relentlessly explores the mind and heart, and I will deal with each of you as you deserve according to your acts" (Revelations 2:23 VOICE); "...appearances don't impress me. I x-ray every motive..." (MSG)

We have to clean up our act. We all fail constantly and have to exercise damage control - for all those conversations we got into - that we wish we hadn't! To make things worse, according to Matthew 12:36 we're going to be held accountable for every idle word: "...people will be called to account for every careless word they have ever said" (VOICE); "...for every empty word."

> It's your heart, not the dictionary that gives meaning to your words... **Every one of these careless words is going to come back to haunt you.** There will be a time of Reckoning. **Words are powerful; take them seriously.** Words can be your salvation. Words can also be your damnation.
>
> (Matthew 12:34-37 MSG)

Our mouths get carried away and leak all kinds of unwanted information. We've all lived in fear of our own mouths before - let's be honest! James 3:6 says that the tongue is a world of trouble: "The tongue also is a fire, a world of evil among the parts of the body. It corrupts the whole body, sets the whole course of one's life on fire, and is itself set on fire by hell." Our tongues often speak for the fallen nature, even more reason to yield that member to the Holy Spirit and His divine nature.

*It only takes a spark, remember, to set off a forest fire. A careless or wrongly placed word out of your mouth can do that. **By our speech we can ruin the world, turn harmony to chaos, throw mud on a reputation,** send the whole world up in smoke and go up in smoke with it, smoke right from the pit of hell.*

(James 3:5-6 MSG)

Are You Manageable?

However, we can talk all day about being good managers but not everyone is willing to be "managed." We must be teachable and pliable if we're to stay on the Potter's wheel as He uses others, such as leadership and parents, to help mould and manage our lives.

The true Body of Christ requires divine administration and so do our individual lives. There's no detail of our lives that the Holy Spirit can't grasp, especially as He numbers every hair on our heads! He governs well, all that's yielded to His control. He must be able to say to us, "You're not in the driver's seat; **I am**" (Matthew 16:24 MSG).

❖

CHAPTER 3

Managing Appetites

Human nature is subject to many appetites [lusts], which must be recognised and managed properly, if we want to serve God correctly. Let's take for example, an appetite for fame and glory [not just chocolate!] This can steer people off course for a lifetime. None of us however, can manage appetites that we're in denial of! We must know them - to be able to manage them!

For example insecurity is an appetite. The need (greed) for acceptance, for attention and appreciation (popularity) can lead us out of the very will of God. "Envy and slander represent a greed for reputation" (Munroe 20). We must not be given to selfish appetites on any level.

This is where fasting becomes relevant, in order to help us subdue such appetites. We must put off their constant nagging, "…**let us strip off and throw aside every encumbrance** (unnecessary weight) and that sin which so readily (deftly and cleverly) clings to and entangles us… Looking away [from all that will distract] to Jesus" (Hebrews 12:1-2 AMP).

Jesus warned against greed most clearly, "**Guard yourselves and keep free from all covetousness** (the immoderate desire for wealth, the greedy longing to have more); for a man's life does not consist in and is not derived from possessing overflowing abundance or that which is over and above his needs" (Luke 12:15-21 AMP).

Jesus continued with this parable about greed:

A wealthy man owned some land that produced a huge harvest. He often thought to himself, "I have a problem here. I don't have anywhere to store all my crops. What should I do? I know! I'll tear down my small barns and build even bigger ones, and then I'll have plenty of storage space for my grain and all my other goods.

Then I'll be able to say to myself, 'I have it made! I can relax and take it easy for years! So I'll just sit back, eat, drink, and have a good time!'" Then God interrupted the man's conversation with himself. "Excuse Me, Mr. Brilliant, but your time has come. Tonight you will die. Now who will enjoy everything you've earned and saved?" **This is how it will be for people who accumulate huge assets for themselves but have no assets in relation to God.**

(Luke 17-21 VOICE)

Poor management has a lot to answer for. On too many occasions, a crisis is the result of someone's greed: "Too much of the time, by default, people let their greed rule their decisions. They do not think about what they are doing. Down the road, their greedy decisions result in a crisis. In a crisis, not only do other people get hurt, often the greedy ones do, too" (Munroe 23).

Greed and generosity are polar opposites. In the parable above Jesus taught us that it's not possible to live for self and for God at the same time: "That's what happens when you fill your barn with Self and not with God" (v21 MSG). It's hard to fill a cup that's already filled [so we must be spilled before we can be filled].

David's Ability to Manage Well

When we look at David pursuing his enemy to get his stuff back [including wives and children] we know that he was not a passive leader who led from the rear. Neither was David greedy. He managed the spoils of war righteously so that everyone got their share and he did not allow it to be hoarded wickedly:

*David came to the 200 men who were so **exhausted and faint** that they could not follow [him] and had been left at the brook Besor [with the baggage]. They came to meet David and those with him, and when he came near to the men, he saluted them. **Then all the wicked and base men** who went with David said, Because they did not go with us, we will give them nothing of the spoil we have recovered, except that every man may lead away his wife and children and depart.*

David said, **You shall not do so, my brethren, with what the Lord has given us.** *He has preserved us and has delivered into our hands the troop that came against us…* **For as is the share of him who goes into the battle, so shall his share be who stays by the baggage. They shall share alike.** *And from that day to this he made it a statute and ordinance for Israel.*

(1 Samuel 30:20-25 AMP)

This is a perfect example of a good leader who knew how to manage his affairs well. Meaning that everyone benefited, not just the few. There was generosity and correct distribution. King David displayed no greed at all, in his actions. In fact leaders, parents, husbands who are motivated by greed, are easily corrupted: "When the righteous are in authority, the people rejoice: but when the wicked beareth rule, the people mourn" (Proverbs 29:2 KJV).

Instead he displayed the ability to manage and administrate righteously. In the book of Acts the need arose for such anointed administration [good management]: **"It is not reason that we should leave the word of God, and serve tables…** look ye out among you seven men of **honest report**, full of the Holy Ghost and wisdom, **whom we may appoint over this business**" (Acts 6:2-3 KJV).

The Keys of the Kingdom

So whether you've been the victim of someone else's greed or just your own, you'll need the strategy of the Holy Spirit to get free of it. Jesus said, "I will give you the **keys of the Kingdom** of heaven…" (Matthew 16:19) That means we've been given access and legal entry. Notice the plural of key. Jesus used the word "keys." We have more than one entry point. There's more than one way to unlock what God has given us. Jesus also said, "The secret of the kingdom of God has been given to you…" (Mark 4:11)

If my house remained locked to me, then all of my possessions would be withheld and I would not be able to benefit from them. **God on the other hand, wants us to have FULL ACCESS to His house and to benefit from His Kingdom here and now.**

Sound management that helps eliminate the chaos in our lives is just one major benefit of the Kingdom.

❖

CHAPTER 4

Our Key to Success

Nothing can unlock a crisis like good management. Bad management on the other hand only expedites a crisis. We've already mentioned in our last chapter that greed and mismanagement are the root causes of most of our problems. And most of us know what a crisis looks like, but what does **sound-management** look like?

According to his book, "Overcoming Crisis," Myles Munroe sights management as the number one key of God's Kingdom: "Management is the effective, efficient, correct and timely use of another person's property and resources for the purpose for which they were delegated with a view to producing the expected added value" (Munroe 39).

Management Defined

Management can be defined by such words as: responsibility, administration, running, managing, organisation; charge, care, direction, leadership, control, governing, governance, ruling, command, superintendence, supervision, overseeing, conduct, handling, guidance, operation. **For example:** "Business improved under the management of new owners."

Every individual on this planet is a manager of something. This is what we have been designed for: "When the Lord God made the earth and filled it up with resources, the very next thing He had to do was to make a manager to take care of it. Men and women were given dominion over the earth's resources. (Notice, however, that they were not given dominion over each other. God was still in charge of the people He had created)" (Munroe 40).

Poor management can apply to very mundane things. For example if you over eat, you gain weight and can seriously compromise your health. Likewise, the job you keep turning up late for, will eventually hang in the balance and the relationships you don't look after will be in jeopardy.

It's all down to management. Good or bad. True management will always protect what has been placed in its oversight. Marriages that are left to ruin will fall apart. Children that are not nurtured will run wild. EVERYTHING in life requires right management for it to thrive and succeed - business, family, health, faith and so on.

Time is not wasted on good management nor are resources; **notice that hoarding is not considered managing.** For example you can hoard and neglect at the same time. Those who manage money invest it; they don't neglect [or bury] it! Why? Because money makes money. Money buried can't earn interest. On the other hand, money that's managed correctly can increase while you sleep! Just as seeds sown in a farmer's field, still grow and germinate while he's sleeping.

There is no Substitute for Training!

Education is so vital, correct knowledge of how to use something enables us to manage it correctly. People specialise in certain things, because they want to manage them properly. Experts exist in almost every field imaginable. We educate ourselves in order to excel in managing specific areas of life. Whether we are managing money in the bank, the stock exchange or managing patients in a hospital, it all comes down to skilful management.

It stands to reason then, that whether we're raising wild horses or educating our own children, we must have the correct know-how in order to manage our affairs properly - regardless. This applies not least to the Body of Christ, where saints must be trained and equipped for works of service (Ephesians 4:12).

No one is exempt from the process of training. Who wants to remain a novice? "My people are destroyed for lack of knowledge..." "My people are ruined because they don't know what's right or true. Because you've turned your back on knowledge, I've turned my back on you..." (Hosea 4:6 KJV; MSG)

Willingness and obedience don't trump training. My six-year-old daughter might want to be a teacher or a dentist one day, but without *proper training*, I'd never let her near my mouth, no matter how much I love her! **There is no substitute for training!** And if we are faithful with little, God will make us faithful over much.

According to the Merriam-Webster online dictionary, sound management is defined as: "the act or skill of controlling and making decisions…" Other descriptions include: "handling, oversight, regulation, keeping, protection, safekeeping, trust, custody and stewardship." Which raises the question, are we owners or just stewards?

Stewardship Vs Ownership

God gives us the ability to be good managers and to be good stewards of what belongs to Him. **Stewards are not owners - but trusted managers of what is placed in their care.** It all belongs to God. In Psalm 115:16 it states,

The heaven of heavens is for God, but he put us in charge of the earth.

(MSG)

Another translation reads,

*The heaven, even the heavens, are the Lord's: but the earth hath he **given** to the children of men.*

(KJV)

However in both the New and Old Testament it clearly states that ownership belongs to God:

The earth is the Lord's, and everything in it.
(1 Corinthians 10:26)

The earth is the Lord's, and the fulness thereof; the world,
and they that dwell therein.
(Psalm 24:1 KJV)

Our role here is to govern, rule and exercise delegated authority to manage everything placed under our care. Basically we are anointed managers, for anointed prosperity on every level.

Again in his book "Overcoming Crisis," Myles Munroe states: "He delegated the management of His creation to the human race and He calls us to account." Therefore it's clear that we are going to have to give account to God for how we managed: "…His money, His time, His gifts, His talents, His resources," including: "the house… the apartment… the car… and more" (Munroe 44).

This means that we are not in a position to claim ownership of anything, especially since "the earth is the Lord's and EVERYTHING in it!" Management is another word for stewardship, which involves accountability and requires responsibility.

Ownership involves possession, rights and title. Where stewardship involves the responsible planning and management of resources. And the concepts of stewardship can be applied to the environment, economics, health, property, information, technology and so on. God can place His stewards in all realms. Even in the scientific arena.

Joseph's Actions always-Elevated People

Joseph is another perfect example of good stewardship. Like David he did not stockpile for personal gain, but for the wider distribution and welfare of others. Through wise management and stewardship, vast resources were gathered - which involved complex logistical strategy, skilful planning and organisation. What was not squandered in a time of plenty, effectively saved lives in a time of crisis.

On the contrary, the rich man mentioned in Luke 12:16-20 stockpiled for himself - Joseph stockpiled for others. Both required years of sound management, skill and hard work - yet one was selfish - the other was service. Ultimately we are caretakers and distributers of God's resources, on this earth. When we fulfil our role of being managers and stewards - as efficiently as Joseph - then everyone benefits and **everyone is elevated above the crisis.**

❖

CHAPTER 5

Don't Jump Ship!

One current example of mismanagement and poor stewardship is the unfortunate events surrounding the cruise ship "Costa Concordia" that was wrecked on 13 January 2012, just off the coast of "Isola del Giglio" on the western coast of Italy (northwest of Rome). As Italy (at present) is my home country, I can testify that this event, never left the headlines for months!

It was the talking point in all the café bars and newspapers. The underlying problem? Mismanagement on behalf of Captain Francesco Schettino, who was eventually sentenced [on February 11, 2015, after a 19-month trial] to 16 years in prison [10 years for manslaughter, five years for causing the shipwreck, and one year for abandoning his passengers].

Although there was also speculation at the time to suggest that he became a convenient fall guy for the Cruise Company "Costa Cruises," (who did eventually disassociate themselves from him!) To make matters worse, Schettino was described as "Italy's most hated man," by the tabloid press and by the end of his trial, Schettino indicated that he'd spent three years, "in a media meat grinder."

Fact: prior to the trial, the chairman of Costa Cruises, put the blame on Captain Schettino and terminated his employment in 2012. The company declined to pay for his legal defence, and eventually became a *co-plaintiff* in the trial against him.

The Result of Mismanagement

This was a very unfortunate incident. His case will no doubt go to appeal; nevertheless, at the time of this writing, the evidence against Captain Schettino does not go largely in his favour!

In fact the order to abandon ship was not issued until *over an hour* after the initial impact. Although international maritime law requires all passengers to be evacuated within 30 minutes of an order to abandon ship, the evacuation of *Costa Concordia* took over **six hours** and not all passengers were evacuated, sadly **32 people in total lost their lives.**

He was accused of multiple manslaughter, for causing a shipwreck, for abandoning the vessel and for failing to contact the authorities when the accident happened.

He was further accused of lying during the trial, as well as in public interviews prior to trial. Prosecutor Stefano Pizza indicated that "**The captain's duty to be the last person off the ship is not just an obligation dictated by ancient maritime rules, it is also a legal obligation intended to limit the damage to those on the ship.**"

Good Managers don't Issue Excuses

However regarding his dry and early departure of the vessel, Schettino had explained that he had *slipped off the ship when it capsized and he had fallen into a lifeboat!* The newspapers helped to fuel disbelief and undermine the credibility of this account, based on pictures of him eating in restaurants shortly afterwards, while the saga continued, when others were still trapped.

The moral of the story is… when we put ourselves first and everyone else last; we violate our role as managers and caretakers. Now unless, this Captain is proven innocent after appeal, this situation will remain a tragedy for *all* involved. No one emerged a winner from this crisis and nobody was elevated. Multiple cases of mismanagement were to blame. Regardless of any scapegoat theory - mismanagement was at the core of this crisis.

Don't Abandon Ship!

We have a lot to learn from this story. And I use this example for more than one reason. **I want to say to my colleagues in leadership - don't jump ship when the going gets tough!** I know that austerity measures are still being felt here in Europe *(at the time of writing this book -2015)* and entire congregations are finding it hard to find employment, an extremely tough environment for many pastors, who are losing most of their best people to greener pastures elsewhere!

Entire congregations are suffering, as People - including their pastors - are jumping ship and leaving with little warning, in hope of finding work.

On a human level I understand this. Having a growing family myself, I can totally appreciate how tough things can get. But this is where our training comes in. This is when we must stand, like Paul urged the believers in Ephesus: "…**stand your ground…** having done all [the crisis demands], to **stand [firmly in your place]**" (Ephesians 6:13 AMP).

> *Be prepared. You're up against far more than you can handle on your own. Take all the help you can get, every weapon God has issued, so that when it's all over but the shouting you'll **still be on your feet.***
>
> *(MSG)*

Where's your Rightful Place?

The question we need to be asking is this: "Where did God call you to live in the first place?" If you're going to, "…stand firmly in your place," you need to know where "your" place is! The anointing is in our lives for the hard stuff! If we are called somewhere specifically, there is always grace and the gift of faith to sustain us there. If not, then I venture to say, that you were never called there in the first place. If greed on the other hand polluted our vision, nothing can sustain the house that's built on sand!

Matthew 6:24 clearly says,

Ye cannot serve God and mammon.

(KJV)

Other translations say,

You must choose one or the other.

(VOICE)

Adoration of one feeds contempt for the other. You can't worship God and Money both.

(MSG)

For example, I was informed the other day of a particular pastor, here in Italy who jumped ship *(without warning)* because he thought his church was sinking! He just got up and left! What about his congregation? [We are responsible before God, if we cause irreversible damage in other people's lives]. Did God call him or not?

No infrastructure whatsoever had been put in place to take care of these people or even help them transition into other local churches. (They were abandoned to a vacuum!) Perhaps we can all agree, this was not God!

Elevate People through their Crisis

So pastors (like any good captain), I urge you to stand your ground and be the LAST to abandon ship! We are accountable before God and we cannot blame the people! And if God directs you to leave, **He would never instruct you to abandon your people without a strategy to elevate them above the crisis.**

As with Joseph, the call of God on our lives as leaders is not for *self-elevation* but for *corporate-elevation*. And we are here to get behind and lift up others, to get them through the crisis. But what does a crisis look like? "In the world you have tribulation *and* trials *and* distress *and* frustration..." (John 16:33 AMP)

If however, we rescue ourselves at the expense of others, this is not Christlike. Jesus rescued others - at the expense of Himself.

Having the right Motives

In the context that we lay down our very lives to serve Christ, then the saying: "The gospel is free, but it's not cheap," is correct. But there are those who actually want to make financial gains from preaching the gospel! I would say however, be careful. Instead think of Joseph, who was second in command only to Pharaoh - in all of Egypt and still did not hoard and amass wealth or success for himself *(this is not what the gifts and call of God are all about).*

Paul the apostle clearly warned about wrong motives and those who, "...**think that godliness is a means to financial gain.**" He went on instead to say that, "...godliness with contentment is great gain" (1 Timothy 6:5-8).

Those who jump ship, simply signed up for the wrong reasons: "I consider everything a loss because of the surpassing worth of knowing Christ Jesus my Lord, for whose sake I have lost all things. I consider them garbage, that I may gain Christ" (Philippians 3:8). This is the true context of *gaining* from the gospel and any hidden greed is always sorely disappointed!

What does Accountability Look Like?

We have received the mandate to manage. To be honourable stewards, who faithfully administrate God's affairs, by the Holy Spirit, here on earth as it is in heaven. In short accountability looks like this:

> *To one servant who had been faithful it was said, "**Well done, good and faithful servant! You have been faithful with a few things; I will put you in charge of many things.** Come and share your master's happiness!" But to the unfaithful servant it was said, "You wicked, lazy servant! …throw that worthless servant outside, into the darkness, where there will be weeping and gnashing of teeth."*
>
> *(Matthew 25:21-30)*

❖

CHAPTER 6

God's Financial Plan

God wants to provide for the Church so that it can do everything it is called to do, something that requires both faith and commitment. Therefore, teaching on tithing and sacrificial giving should be available to each member.

The Truth about Tithing

I heard a very prominent preacher recently on TV telling his congregation, "The devil can only operate in what you don't know, and that is why I must keep teaching on money, tithing, offering and giving. You cannot afford to remain ignorant and I must keep you informed so that the devil cannot use your ignorance." I found his rather blunt statements interesting in reference to John 8:32, which says, "You will know the truth, and the truth will set you free."

The entrance and unfolding of Your words give light; their unfolding gives understanding (discernment and comprehension)...

(Psalm 119:130 AMP)

Obviously the emphasis here is on the word "know" because without the "knowledge" of truth, that same truth cannot affect us. Therefore it can only be the truth that we "know" personally (by revelation) that can set us free. In fact our personal and individual knowledge of the truth is so crucial, that it keeps the enemy working tirelessly to keep us ignorant of the truth or at best, to distort it.

And in that context, I must agree with my fellow preacher; we do indeed have a responsibility to keep heralding "truth" - over and over again - in order to keep ignorance at bay. We have a responsibility to preach with the Spirit of revelation and not just "information" so that people can really "receive" the truth. Adding to that, any teacher in training will inform you, that the "art of teaching is in *repetition!*"

Yes! Tithing is still Relevant

Tithing and giving in general are fundamental to our faith. And it's important for every church member to understand that God alone is our source and supply, our provider who is generous, able and willing to bless us financially. Jesus said plainly in Luke 6:38, "Give and it will be given to you." In other words, God meets our needs, when we meet the needs of others: "Whoever sows generously will reap generously" (2 Corinthians 9:6).

No church member should ever feel that they have been exploited or coerced into giving money. It must be voluntary. There must be understanding, faith and revelation that God will bless and help us in every way, including the financial realm. Therefore biblical teaching about tithing and giving is not just empty words, but a precious revelation that we must nurture and keep alive in this culture of greed!

When we as believers understand our service in this area, financial blessings are then released over our personal lives and that of our families, ministries and churches.

Sometimes we have heard pastors say out of frustration: "What we need are three or four millionaires to pay our bills." Or alternatively, "Where are all the businessmen?" But how wrong that is! Three millionaires are *not* necessary. First what is necessary is "faith" in the pastor's heart. Second we need correct teaching that builds "faith" in the people and results in commitment. Furthermore it was never intended that a few members should carry the whole financial burden; everyone should share the weight.

What is simpler than the fact that God wants everyone to love Him? And as Ulf Ekman once said, "Everyone should praise Him. All should be intercessors. All should go out with the gospel and all should be givers. This gives strength to a believer's ministry. God does not only want specialists whom we can admire. He seeks an entire group who can rise up, pay the price of commitment and walk with Him. Then great power is released."

He went on to say, "God wants everyone to give to His work: 'Each man should give what he has decided in his heart to give.' God expects every active believer to be a giver," (Ekman, The Church of the Living God 101).

Instigated by God

What we need to perceive properly is that God, not by man, instigated tithing. Even before the Law, Abraham and Jacob gave a tenth of everything (Genesis 14:20, 28:22). The principle of tithing is found throughout the bible. Jesus spoke about it in Matthew 23:23, where He emphasised righteousness and compassion, but **tithing was not to be exempt. You should not do one thing and overlook the other.**

The book of Hebrews also speaks about tithing (Hebrews 7:2-9). In Malachi 3:6-12, God emphasised that a tenth belongs to Him and that it should be brought into the storehouse. **The storehouse can be any Christian church, ministry or organisation where one receives food and nourishment.**

God instructs that we Test Him

Therefore ten percent of our income belongs to God, which simply means that **we manage better on 90 percent with God's blessings, than on 100 percent without God's blessing!** Why? Because when we do not give our tithe, we are robbing God of something that belongs to Him; the tenth does not belong to us, it belongs to God.

Giving a tenth to God means that we are surrendering, sanctifying and circumcising our income so that we can safely stand in His covenant where we can count on His blessings; only then is heaven open over us: "Bring the whole tithe into the storehouse, that there may be food in my house. Test me in this," says the Lord Almighty, "and see if I will not throw open the floodgates of heaven and pour out so much blessing that you will not have room enough for it" (Malachi 3:10).

Finally: tithing puts us in a position of protection and blessing. It is God's perfect Financial Plan! Why would He create structure in everything else but leave the subject of money to our random (individual) discretion?

His Kingdom and His Body are meant to be in complete order, with no chaos and no anarchy. His perfect plan for our well-being, includes tithing. Once we accept this, the easier we make it for ourselves! Because our heart is always where our treasure is, and surely our hearts belong to God. Tithing is just our opportunity to prove it; where we demonstrate our faithfulness and commitment to Him in every single area of our lives, including our money!

Seed Sowing doesn't Trump Tithing

God has destined us all to be "seed sowers," from Eden right until now but before we get into that, first it must be said that **all giving must be preceded by the tithe**, because seed sowing does not cancel out or trump the need to tithe. In fact tithing must always come before giving (seed sowing). In fact it is the foundation of all seed sowing. If your seed does not bring you a harvest, check your tithe, because you can't forget to tithe. (Your seed can't bypasses your tithe).

Failing to be faithful with your tithe will hinder your seed. **Make sure you tithe as a priority and then follow**

with your seed; be careful to sow plentiful seed! But don't waste your precious seed by failing to tithe first.

Tithing is the Foundation of Spiritual Blessing

Notice in Malachi that tithes and offerings come together, but one precedes the other. The tithe comes first, then the seed, then the harvest. This is God's order. In other words, to sow and expect a harvest without first tithing, will make your seed ineffective. Tithing is the foundation of spiritual blessing. As with all architecture, the simple rule is this: no foundation, no building, *(unless you want a tent!)*

> *Will a man rob or defraud God? Yet you rob and defraud*
> *Me. But you say, In what way do we rob or defraud You?*
> *[You have withheld your] tithes and offerings. You are*
> *cursed with the curse, for you are robbing Me...*
> *(Malachi 3:8-9)*

Once you have settled this about tithing in your heart then all is set and in place. **But neither is tithing alone enough in itself** (there is more than one principle about money!) Once you have tithed then your seeds must be sown and then you must have **a lifestyle of constant giving** (after all true living is in our giving!)

Our Lifestyle can't Consist of Giving like Heaven and Living like Hell!

> *God, your God, is the God of all gods, he's the Master of*
> *all masters, a God immense and powerful and awesome.*
> *He doesn't play favourites, **takes no bribes,** makes sure*

orphans and widows are treated fairly, takes loving care of
foreigners by seeing that they get food and clothing.
(Deuteronomy 10:17 MSG)

Lifestyle is very important. Because some people treat the tithe like they can use it to pay God off! God can't be bribed or bought. Too many people think that they can "give like heaven and live like hell!" When tithing should be a response to our faith in God.

Not many people are aware of this fact, but **John Lennon** used to believe in tithing! And would tithe ten percent of his entire income, (to different causes, as he believed it was the best way to save the world!) He revealed this in an infamous Playboy interview back in 1980, when he announced: **"Anybody I want to save will be helped through our tithing, which is ten percent of whatever we earn,"** (Playboy Interview with John Lennon and Yoko Ono, Copyright © 1980 Playboy Press, http://www.whale.to/b/lennon1.html).

Tithing by Faith not The Law

Clearly, tithing alone is not enough, (on its own merits). Certainly in the New Covenant, like all else, **tithing must be an act of faith and not law.** We know that Abraham's tithing for instance, was free of the law, because he gave a tenth [tithe means ten], 400 years **before the law** (Genesis 14:20). We give our tenth by faith because we come **after the law!**

Now I don't want to risk oversimplifying this, but those worshiping Mammon today (the spirit of money), fiercely defend their right not to tithe (using the law as their main argument!) How then can they rationalise Abraham's tithing, which was completely **untouched** by the law?

If Abraham could tithe by faith then, we certainly can tithe by faith now! In fact Romans 10:17 in the King James Version says, "Whatsoever is not of faith is sin…" Other translations read: "Any action not consistent with faith is sin" (VOICE); "If the way you live isn't consistent with what you believe, then it's wrong," (MSG). **Therefore we have no business doing ANYTHING without faith, especially tithing!**

Jesus: The New Covenant

For the sake of argument about whether tithing is relevant to the New Testament or not, let's turn to Luke 11:42 where Jesus Himself is speaking and encouraging tithing:

> *Woe to you Pharisees, because you give God a tenth of your mint, rue and all other kinds of garden herbs, but you neglect justice and the love of God. You should have practiced the latter **without leaving the former undone**…*

> *(see also Matthew 23:23)*

Jesus said, **"…you should not have left the former [referring to the tithe] undone."** Some people however, try and discount this; by saying that Jesus was in the Old Covenant, therefore everything that He taught was Old Covenant! Yes Jesus may have lived in the Old Covenant but He was not **"under"** the Old Covenant. Jesus fulfilled (ratified) the Old and brought (was the mediator) of the New; but more than that - **HE WAS THE NEW COVENANT!**

We know this because He said, "'This is my body, which is for you...' In the same way, after supper he took the cup, saying, **'This cup IS THE NEW COVENANT IN MY BLOOD...'"** (1 Corinthians 11:24-25). [See also Hebrews 7:22; 8:6; 9:15; 12:24].

Giving is Releasing and the 1st Principle of Increase

One person gives freely, yet gains even more; another withholds unduly, but comes to poverty. A generous person will prosper; whoever refreshes others will be refreshed. People curse the one who hoards grain, but they pray God's blessing on the one who is willing to sell.
(Proverbs 11:24-26)

With God, **"releasing"** is the first principle of increase but with man of course, it is the exact opposite! The natural man enjoys "hoarding" and "holding onto" in order to have plenty. But if we read the scripture in the Message bible it says: "The world of the generous gets larger and larger; the world of the stingy gets smaller and smaller. The one who blesses others is abundantly blessed; those who help others are helped."

The message here is clear, that in God's economy it's the "generous" who gain the richest returns, (so that they can give again and give more!) Whereas those who hoard-

greedily, "reduce" themselves to their own limitations (and "decrease" in value!) One operates in the blessing; the other operates in the curse.

> *So let each one give as he purposes in his heart, not grudgingly or of necessity; for God loves a cheerful giver. And God is able to make all grace abound toward you, that you, having all sufficiency in all things, have an abundance for every good work.*
>
> *(2 Corinthians 9:7 NKJV)*

> *As it is written, "He has dispersed abroad, He has given to the poor; His righteousness remains forever." Now may He who supplies seed to the sower, and bread for food, supply and **multiply the seed you have sown** and increase the fruits of your righteousness, while you are enriched in everything for all liberality, which causes thanks giving through us to God.*
>
> *(2 Corinthians 9:6-11)*

Seeds Must be Sown before they can Multiply

Notice how it says, "…multiply the seed you have sown." Using the past tense to imply that only the seed that *has been sown* can be multiplied. Seed that has not been sown yet cannot bring a harvest, the same way that seeds in a box cannot grow until they have been planted!

Pastor Ulf Ekman said, "Whether you sow your time, your money or something else, you will always reap the same thing that you sow. This is how it works in the natural: parsley seed does not produce carrots. It is impossible. What you put in the ground is exactly what comes up" (Ekman, Financial Freedom 113-114).

Another facet of this law is that some crops grow quickly, while others take more time. This can be both good and bad. The person who plants an olive tree seldom lives long enough to pick an olive from the same tree. **In this case it is the next generations that will reap what the previous one has planted.** Certain things bring long-term results, while other things produce a quick, but un-enduring return.

When you plant or sow something, it is better to find a seed that continues to produce fruit for a long period of time. For example, we will benefit more from the seed of an apple tree than from the seed of a radish. God has provided us with long-term areas in which to sow and He will show us exactly what they are.

The Law of Sowing and Reaping

Paul tells us that he who sows sparingly will also reap sparingly. But to encourage us, he also promises: "And God is able to make all grace abound toward you, that you, always having all sufficiency in all things, may have an abundance for every good work."(2 Corinthians 9:8 NKJV) Here, God is saying that **He is the giver and we are the sowers. He supplies seed to the sower and bread for food. If we dare to place ourselves at His disposal and begin to give, this law will come into operation.**

We need to remember two important laws: **the law of sowing and reaping** and **the law of faith.** We must always walk in faith, and to exercise faith by beginning to sow what little seed we have. Taking just one step of faith at a time, especially when we have very little to give, or sow.

We must begin by doing something, if this law is to function for us. At a time of need it is easy to think that we ought to hold on to what we have. The mentality of the world says, "Keep what you have. Don't let anyone else have it." However, the Kingdom of God says the opposite!

Giving is Obedience

This law of sowing and reaping works. If we dare to test it, God will give us more blessings than we have room to contain. We must make a *quality* decision to always do what God tells us to do. Every time we wonder if we can afford it, we are asking our chequebook for permission! If God says yes and our chequebook says no, do it anyway. On the other hand we should not do anything if God says no, even if your chequebook says yes! **We must be led by the Holy Spirit and not by our bank balance!**

If God exhorts us to sow into a particular project, we must not delay. **When the Holy Spirit speaks, we should be prepared to sow within a second's notice.** This will bring us out of financial bondage and into freedom, where God wants everyone of us to be. If we lack money at the moment, God will provide it. There is no greater satisfaction than to give to the work of God. It involves being independent of the world and having the freedom to act and do what God has told us to do.

When Paul exhorts the Corinthians to contribute to the collection for the poor in Jerusalem, he uses the substitutionary death of Jesus as a motivation for them to give. According to Paul, the reason they should give is because Christ Jesus Himself became poor so that, through His poverty, they might become rich (2 Corinthians 8:9-14).

And he shall be like a tree firmly planted [and tended] by the streams of water, ready to bring forth its fruit in its season; its leaf also shall not fade or wither; and everything he does shall prosper [and come to maturity].
(Psalm 1:3 AMP)

❖

CHAPTER 7

Underground Cash Economy

In the world's system, referring to whatever country we are resident, it is only *right* and *legal* that we *contribute to the welfare* of our respective countries. In fact our country of origin would not survive without a clear structure or system that really works. In the west we call this democracy and there are many different forms of democracy.

> *God doesn't stir us up into confusion; he brings us into harmony.*
>
> (1 Corinthians 14:33 MSG)

Why would it not survive? Because living without structure is like living without a backbone! A society without structure or backbone is a lawless society governed and driven by dominant *law-lords* rather than a system that looks out for the genuine welfare of its citizens. Rather than just letting the strongest survive... it's fairness for all. That is the aim of democracy no matter how flawed it is and included in this pursuit of "fairness" is the necessity to pay taxes; which in turn "maintains" the overall system.

Various economies would be quite manageable if everyone contributed to the systems that have been established through these governments. I'm talking about democratic societies.

Jeffrey Grant gives some staggering figures about what he calls the **"Underground Cash Economy."** He says, "The greatest problem facing the government is their desperate need to generate additional tax revenues" (Jeffrey 105). Doesn't this sound like the Church? And yet we don't need additional tax, what we need is additional tithes!

Mr. Grant goes on to say, "Huge welfare costs and massive interest payments on the national debt have created staggering deficits. However, the resistance of voters to higher taxes has put the government in a difficult position. Studies reveal a huge amount of the economic and financial transactions are not being recorded or taxed at all. Increasingly, people are using cash in an attempt to escape high taxes" (Jeffrey 105).

Over the last decades various studies have shown that the untaxed underground economies of separate countries are estimated to be well into the billions! With figures for the US economy much higher, even into the trillions each year; however if a significant part of this underground economy was taxed, budget deficits would disappear and governments would be able to begin paying off their national debts. In fact some economists estimate that one third of the economy escapes taxation!

Each government has to decide how to distribute this funding that is generated through these various taxes, for the welfare of its society. With democratically elected leadership, who have authority *(locally and nationally)*, and the responsibility to make the right decisions on behalf of its society.

I believe what God wants us to understand and reflect on such facts and figures so that the Body of Christ can rectify the error of perhaps more than 80% of its members, who make the poor decision "not to tithe" and yet still think that God's Kingdom here on this earth will somehow supernaturally exist without the responsibility of its own people. "There is no shortage of finance..."one economist said, "...in fact there are enough resources in this world for everyone to be a millionaire!"

Consider our National Insurance contributions and pension schemes that are paid or given on behalf of one's self and one's own family's welfare or well being. These payments *(in most cases)* bring about personal returns.

On thinking about such things God spoke to me one night and gave me a revelation that His Kingdom operates in much the same way. In fact a lot of what we have in society has been taken and established out of a spiritual kingdom. The difference is of course that man is in control of one system, (we call this the Babylonian system) and God is in control of the other!

Because of the fall of mankind, much of our earthly system is influenced by greed and the love of money or stuff. But these attitudes don't just exist within our society the Church also is infested with much of the same spirit!

Finally when it comes to tithing and giving offerings, we are ultimately free to decide what we do with our money, although our flesh usually wins every time! It is those living and operating out of their spirit and not their flesh that are successfully led to do the right thing. At the end of the day everything belongs to the Lord, all the time that He is in control there is no chaos.

God is not the author of confusion, spiritual or financial. The question then is: **"Why do bad things happen to good people?"** And in a similar way, why do faithful people suffer lack? Usually there is a link in the chain that has been severed. God has called us to be united and to work together in one accord. After all we are in the same Kingdom!

If only a small percentage of Kingdom dwellers know how to operate in their finances as the Holy Spirit leads, imagine how much easier things would be if everyone else did their part as well!

The Aaron's Tithe of the Tithe!

Give these instructions to the Levites: When you receive from the people of Israel the tithes I have assigned as your allotment, give a tenth of the tithes you receive-a tithe of the tithe-to the Lord... You must present one-tenth of the tithe received from the Israelites as a sacred offering to the Lord. This is the Lord's sacred portion, and you must present it to Aaron the priest. Be sure to give to the Lord the best portions of the gifts given to you.

(Numbers 18:26-29 NLT)

One of the questions that I had for many years regarding finance was in relation to "Does a leader need to tithe the tithe?" The answer to this is found in the above scripture, Numbers 18:26-29. The Levite priests were commanded to pay a tithe from the tithe that they received from the people and give it to Aaron. We can call this, "The Aaron's Tithe."

Out of interest the same Scripture in the Message bible reads:

When you get the tithe from the People... **you must tithe that tithe and present it as an offering to God. Your offerings will be treated the same as other people's gifts...***This is your procedure for making offerings to God* **from all the tithes you get from the People... give God's portion from these tithes to Aaron the priest. Make sure that God's portion is the best... and holiest of everything you get.**

(Numbers 18:26-29)

And we see very clearly that the priests lived off of the tithe, something that we must be clear about in our teaching when we teach on the subject of *Anointed Prosperity*. Then in regard to church leadership, pastors and directors of Christian organisations or apostolic networks, the principle remains the same; that if we teach one thing and then excuse ourselves because of our preference and position - this is completely hypocritical.

Many pastors of churches give offerings *(but they don't necessarily tithe)* - like for example towards the random itinerant ministry gifts that come through and minister in their churches, including towards their own structural developments and outreach projects. Now of course these things are wonderful but it is not what God was instructing in Numbers 18:26-29; and such "gifts" are geared to sure up one's own agenda rather than giving the best and holiest to God, which is what tithing for leaders on this level is all about.

Now developing the vision that God has given us is not wrong in itself, nor is it wrong encouraging our members to give into certain projects that in turn will enhance them. And yes teaching our people to tithe and give offerings into the storehouse so that there is meat in God's house and an open heaven is all good. On the other hand however when you step back and look at this theory, superficially it all looks wonderful when actually it is also teetering over the trap of deception.

For instance I believe that in these end times not only will there be a greater development of networking, where ministries are concerned, but also the network of fathering via the Apostolic Ministry. It's important to remain connected, committed and under the right structural covering. For example every leader or pastor needs to be in a relationship that is accountable in an apostolic way.

And while it's important to teach our lay people all about tithing we, as organisational leaders, ministries and churches ought also to be tithing faithfully to God through *"tithing the tithe"* to those whom God has specifically connected us to apostolically speaking.

As leaders we are not "exempt" from tithing, rather we should be "exemplary" in it by **giving tithe to the Aaron that God has specifically placed in our lives.** So this is where we place the tithe of the tithe - not to random ministries or events (that flow in and out of our lives without accountability).

When we tithe in a correct manner, we are tithing the best of the best "unto the Lord." And to this you might say, *"well I'm connected and in relationship with so many!"* While this might be correct, ask yourself, of all those you are "connected to," who is your Pastor or Apostle? Who has been assigned to be an Aaron in your life?

This is something that has to be settled between you and God and not something you can change or rearrange, *(like the goal posts)* when it suits you! Again the question has to be asked, "Whom do you ultimately submit to, besides the Lord? Who represents God in your life? Who can speak for Him when you are not seeing straight?"

We are discussing a certain person in your life who goes beyond mere acquaintance or friendship; someone who has a "voice" into your life, a voice that holds considerable "weight" when it really matters. Whoever that person is, then this is where you should be tithing your tithe *(the best and holiest part of everything given to you, v29)* to honour the Lord. And I don't mean your wage; I mean 10% of the income of the WHOLE of your ministry or church. Re-read Numbers where it says "the best of everything."

I stress this is not an idea of mine that I have stumbled across, nor is it an effort to conjure up finances for my own ministry! As much as I relish the support, I am rather forced to correct an "incorrectness" that exists in the Body, by addressing this subject and using very clear scriptural evidence to do so, which very often gets swept under the religious proverbial carpet!

We often conveniently sidestep such issues, especially those that threaten our personal economy and create a levy upon our finances!

But if we will obey scripture on this point, then this will not only release an open heaven over our personal lives as ministers but will also flow down through every branch of our Vision *(it is our tithe that opens up the floodgates.)* And then of course our offerings that go to those random itinerant ministries on occasion can still bring a harvest of supply to our ministries and churches that will positively affect all of our people, only then will we be living what we teach.

Let me finish this chapter with this; as I travel I find that some pastors have the attitude, that their ministry should be the only ministry within the church that should receive a wage! To that I ask another question: *"IS THIS GOD'S WAY?"* I don't believe it is. Because what that creates is various "ministry gifts" starting churches only so that they can finance their ministry! They play the role of a pastor to pacify the notion that this is the only way to fund their real identity and what they are truly called to do!

People have hidden behind the safe title of "Pastor" for generations because it is unassuming and less offensive. Nevertheless it is unscriptural for "everyone" to be a Pastor! They shouldn't have to relinquish their true identities and callings within the Body, just to fit an easier and more acceptable mould. It's ludicrous and only with a restoration of all-things-apostolic can these haphazard notions be lifted. It has caused internal restrictions within the Body of Christ, not allowing gifts to function as they should and as God designed them; for the best functioning and benefit of the whole Body.

Clearly then what is really needed is a return towards the apostolic, where apostolic teams work together within the Body, and where all the five fold gifts are recognised and enhance one another in order to create a balanced ministry for the people. With a financial structure capable of supporting it, with regular income that allows each "gift" to thrive and not just "survive" in the wrong positions. God has made every provision for us to be successful and to remain so.

My ministry motto for many years has always been; **"His voice is all the provision you need"** based on the 28th chapter of Deuteronomy. Every instruction we need, is in His Word. If we fall short, it is only because we have negated His Logos or His Rhema and have failed to obey it!

❖

CHAPTER 8

Alms, A Vital Decision

In this chapter you will discover God's heart towards the topic of "alms-deeds." A very weighty topic indeed, because **generosity to the poor is what helps separate the men from the boys, when it comes to true Christianity or should we say discipleship!** In Acts 9:36 we see one particular disciple remembered famously for her alms-deeds: "Now there was at Joppa a certain disciple named Tabitha, which by interpretation is called Dorcas: this woman was full of good works and **alms-deeds** which she did" (KJV); "...she was always doing good and helping the poor."

So close to God's heart in fact, is our treatment of the poor and distressed, that our own eternal destiny might actually hang in the balance because of it:

*Then he will say to those on his left, "Depart from me, you who are **cursed,** into the eternal fire prepared for the devil and his angels. **For I was hungry and you gave me noting to eat, I was thirsty and you gave me nothing to drink, I was a stranger and you did not invite me in, I needed clothes and you did not clothe me, I was sick and in prison and you did not look after me."***

*They also will answer, "Lord, when did we see you hungry or thirsty or a stranger or needing clothes or sick or in prison, and did not help you?" He will reply, **"I tell you the truth, whatever you did not do for one of the least of these, you did not do for me."** Then they will go away to eternal punishment, but the righteous to eternal life.*

(Matthew 25:41-46)

As much as many of us have confessed on Jesus as Lord and Saviour and have considered ourselves the beneficiaries of eternal life, have we ever really perceived this scripture in its entirety?

Yes salvation is a result of confessing on Jesus Christ as our Lord and Saviour - but this goes beyond something we do as mere form and practice - our whole lifestyle must change.

Part of being Christlike *(having His divine nature)* is reaching out to those in need, giving alms and being actively involved in caring for the poor. It may not be our entire ministry focus but it must be our attitude and way of life regardless. And as we focus on godly management in our lives, alms-giving has to be a legitimate and strategic part of this overall subject: **"Kingdom Management for Anointed Prosperity."**

Prophetically speaking, I would say, that over the next few years, a much sharper divide is going to emerge, between those that have and those that don't have. Yes, wealth is on the increase, just as the bible declares, but also poverty is on the increase, as with many other developments that are taking place.

There is also a great movement of unrest in the earth right now. For example statistics show that as boarders have been relaxed in places such as Europe specifically, more than ever before, multitudes are on the move - looking for a better life. However Jesus told His disciples, that we would always have the poor amongst us; unfortunately poverty also brings crime.

People do not despise a thief if he steals to satisfy his hunger when he is starving. Yet if he is caught, he must pay sevenfold, though it costs him all the wealth of his house.

(Proverbs 6:30-31)

I remember one of my first trips to Nigeria, West Africa, where the local army arranged with the police to have me stopped outside of the airport - in the middle of the night - putting their guns through the window of my taxi and said, *"We want your money...!"* That is what poverty does to people. It drives them to a place of despair, to a place of crime.

As frightening and as vulnerable as this situation was, I remember recognising that these men weren't looking to get rich. They weren't being greedy; *they were looking merely to survive.* Why? Because these soldiers had not been paid for 6 months! There is no excuse to validate stealing, yet how else were they to feed their families? God's heart is one of LOVE, COMPASSION AND GENEROSITY. And He is looking to reach out through us.

Now a self-preservationist is a person who only looks to meet his own needs. However I am not suggesting that our giving should get out of hand, by doing silly things that jeopardise our safety or that we should compulsively give out of what we don't have, (so as to cause debt and a bad witness), surely not! However, I do suggest that we should rather approach every situation, from the leading of the Holy Spirit. Then we will hit the mark every time, without casting our precious pearls before swine. Instead our giving will be on time and provoke much praise towards heaven; exceeding all those fleshly endeavours and guilt-motivated, random hits and misses!

My wife always looks to give strategically to people in need. It's something she strongly feels God has spoken to her about. For example, in Italy there are many Moroccan women begging on the streets (who use their children as **emotional-bate** to capture the hearts of the passerby). To remedy this, my wife began buying little cakes and drinks for these children, as well as the mothers. [Many times she couldn't give more and felt this was God's directive].

She told me once: "They try to thank me, but I'm not asking for anything in return. However if I do get anything from it... it's always the big bright smiles I get flashed from the children... it says absolutely everything!"

Giving this way also means that you are treating beggars like human beings, looking them in the eye and telling them God loves them. It provides us with the opportunity to witness for Christ. Don't pity them or judge them... just give to them what they need (as is possible) and then walk away.

It's their responsibility what they do with it afterwards. Don't control them with your giving! And don't suppose that your gift is insignificant either, just because it's not rocket-size! This type of thinking stops you from giving. They are not asking for a Ferrari! Just give something. Ask the Holy Spirit. Find a way to refresh their soul. Don't wait. Don't excuse yourself any further just: **"Stop. Love. Act."**

Everyone in the city of Florence is aware that these women are being forced to beg by their own husbands, who pimp them and their families on the streets! My wife and I once found their meeting place and watched as they re-grouped and re-organised (with the men gathering the money). Yes, they are breaking the law and at times I've even said to my wife, "Some of those guys have more money than we do...!" But that's never the issue; God just tells us all to GIVE. And we've already seen in Matthew (25:34-46) that our own **salvation rests upon it...!**

If we only tithe and give offerings without giving alms to the poor - it has to be said and this is a serious subject - our selfishness could be an issue at the **judgment seat of Christ** whether we get into heaven or not! Refusing to help others puts us in a dangerous place, where God's Word already judges us. **However we must not forget that God expects us to give alms "alongside" our tithe and offerings, we can't do one while neglecting the other.**

Greek for *"alms"* - *eleemosune,* (also connected with *eleemon* - see Strong's 1654) means: *"merciful,"* signifies (a) *"mercy, pity, particularly in giving alms,"* Matthew 6:1, 2-4; Acts 10:2; 24:17; (b) the benefaction itself, the *"alms" (the effect for the cause),* Luke 11:41; 12:33; Acts 3:2-3, 10; 9:36, *"alms-deeds;"* 10:2, 4, 31. Note: In Matthew 6:1, the RV, translating *dikaiosune,* according to the most authentic texts, has *"righteousness,"* for KJV, *"alms."*

If we put God first, He will prove Himself. On the other hand, how can we ever expect God to bless and prosper us if we do not heed the cry of the poor and be merciful? **"If a man shuts his ears to the cry of the poor, he too will cry out and not be answered" (Proverbs 21:13).** And in Acts 20:35 Paul says:

> *In everything I did, I showed you that by this kind of hard work we must help the weak, remembering the words the Lord Jesus himself said:* **It is more blessed to give than to receive.***"*
>
> *(see also 2 Corinthians 8:9-15)*

God will meet our needs if we meet the needs of others. As we learn to give to the poor, God will bless our lives. However if we neglect this area then we have neglected **one of the most important principles of God's Ways of Financial Increase.**

The Cold Indifference and Self-indulgence of our Culture

Those who give to the poor will lack nothing, but those who **close their eyes** *to them receive many curses.*
(Proverbs 28:27)

I wonder if you fully realise the charge that God issued against Sodom? It might come as a surprise to you, but has everything to do with the poor! In Ezekiel 16:19 the Lord compares Jerusalem with Sodom, by saying: "Behold, this was the iniquity of your sister Sodom: **pride, overabundance of food, prosperous ease,** *and* **idleness... neither did she strengthen the hand of the poor and needy"** (Ezekiel 16:49 AMP). "The sin of your sister Sodom was this: She lived... in the lap of luxury — **proud, gluttonous, and lazy. They ignored the oppressed and the poor"** (MSG).

Further to this, in his book, "Orphans, Widows, the Poor and Oppressed," Derek Prince claimed that there was no mention of any sexual vice in the charge against her because "...the basic sins of Sodom were; **selfishness, carnality, self-indulgence and looking after number one..."** And again he went on to say, "The sins of our day are just like the sins of Sodom... **the root is selfishness, self-indulgence, indifference to others"** (Prince 17-19).

This is a radical concept. However does this mean that God is indifferent towards sexual vice then? No! Of course not. But what this does reveal, is just how high on God's agenda, our treatment of the poor and oppressed is. Sometimes we get sidetracked by all the headlines, that we forget what's most important in the very heart of God. "Whoever is kind to the poor lends to the Lord, and he will reward them for what they have done" (Proverbs 19:17); "…will be repaid in full *and with interest*" (VOICE).

Here's a short selection of the many verses concerning our treatment of the poor and needy:

- "Whoever mocks the poor shows contempt for their Maker" (Proverbs 17:5).

- "Do not oppress the widow or the fatherless, the foreigner or the poor" (Zechariah 7:10).

- "You're here to defend the defenceless, to make sure that underdogs get a fair break; Your job is to stand up for the powerless, and prosecute all those who exploit them" (Psalm 82:3-4 MSG).

- "Blessed is he that considereth the poor: the Lord will deliver him in time of trouble" (Psalm 41:1 KJV).

Finally in James 2:1-4 it says:

*My dear friends, don't let public opinion influence how you live out our glorious, Christ-originated faith. If a man enters your church wearing an expensive suit, and a **street person wearing rags** comes in right after him, and you say to the man in the suit, "Sit here, sir; this is the best seat in the house!" and either ignore the street person or say, "Better sit here in the back row," **haven't you segregated God's children and proved that you are judges who can't be trusted?***

(MSG)

So our job is not to **judge** or be **indifferent** towards the needs of others, (unconcerned, apathetic and void of sympathy), but to reveal God's love to them at every opportunity. Next time you see someone begging in the street, show God's love in action, (because love looks like something). And instead of judging or showing cold indifference towards their plight, simply ask the Holy Spirit for wisdom: **"Lord, what's on your heart... how can I help... what can I give?"**

Our responsibility is to **give,** not to judge. I must say, that I chuckle when people appear so critically concerned about what happens to their ten pence (it's nothing but loose change!) Perhaps we should say to such individuals, "Don't be deluded; no one can get drunk (or high) on your ten pence! Don't allow that mean spirit of indifference to block your compassion or stop your giving, be free to love these people, in Jesus name!"

❖

CHAPTER 9

Appropriating God's Word

As we pray over our gifts, again we must do what the late Derek Prince advised, and **appropriate God's Word.** We must **"say"** something agreeable-with or in affirmation-to the scriptures, in the process of our giving. It is **as we give** that we need to employ faith; this is paramount. It took effort for the Queen of Sheba to do what she did, it was not a passing thought, instead it was completely deliberate.

When the queen of Sheba heard of Solomon's fame, she came to Jerusalem to test him with hard questions. She arrived with a large group of attendants and a great caravan of camels loaded with spices, large quantities of gold, and precious jewels. When she met with Solomon, she talked with him about everything she had on her mind.

(2 Chronicles 9:1 NLT)

Giving is just one part of this, faith is the other all-important part that legitimises our gift and brings the results of our giving right-back-at-us! See it like this, faith fertilises our seed, just like sperm the egg or bees the flowers! **Everything hangs on that faith connection, in the Kingdom of God (especially if we expect to see Kingdom anointed prosperity!)**

One example of a prayer we could pray over our seed is this:

"God, I want to be a part of this... therefore I am deliberately going to sow part of my life into this particular person's life and ministry. As I activate my faith, I also ask You Father to open doors of access, that allow the same blessings that exist on their life, to flow toward me, so that I too can be more effective for Your Kingdom, Amen."

Faith is Deliberate

Nothing happens on autopilot in the Kingdom of God - we have to be deliberate about our faith. Our faith alone activates the things of God. **Faith is always the prerequisite**. Often we believe that everything about God is unconditional, but it is His love alone that is unconditional, everything else about Him is totally conditional!

The biggest condition of all is the **FAITH CONDITION**, which is attached to everything that God is: "…without faith it is impossible to please Him" (Hebrews 11:6 NKJV).

Like the queen of Sheba gave gifts in order to see things happen in her own life, we must NEVER NEGLECT to mix faith with our giving. We must never waste good seed or good gifts by failing to activate our faith alongside them. **Wasted or misguided giving cannot please God.**

Divine Reciprocation

However we must not miss one vital element here. Obviously we can't get from someone what he or she is not able to give, in terms of anointing or impartation. **So where we give and what we give, does determine our return**. The Queen of Sheba needed something that none of her peers could give her, so she drew close to the one who could, King Solomon. Again, it wasn't just a selfish desire; it was reciprocal. It was very important to her that she could better serve the people of her realm and to fulfil her role as queen. We could say that she was "equipping herself."

The same applies to us, if we need something (a particular quality that we see in others), that will better help us to fulfil our God given role, then we too must give purposefully and receive purposefully, just as she did. We must never throw anything to chance and call it faith! That is anything BUT.

Faith on the other hand is determined and purposeful and our giving must match that. God is not aimless when it comes to our lives; He determines that we have, "…a hope and a future and an expected end," (Jeremiah 29:11). Likewise in Romans 8:28 it says we are, "…called according to His purpose." There are no accidents in the Kingdom of God. **Our giving should NEVER take on the status of an accident. It should be deliberate, intentional and directed. Throwing things up in the air and seeing where they land is NOT FAITH.** Especially when it comes to our giving.

Yes! We must allow the Lord to convict our hearts regards giving into certain ministries, churches or Christian organisations, especially those whom God has used the most to help nourish, nurture and feed us spiritually. We should and we must sow, in order to partake of the blessing and anointing that is upon their lives. This is God's plan - for us to sow and to reap - in **"divine reciprocation."**

They *(ministries)* too are part of this divine reciprocation. They labour and toil and sacrifice in order to bring us the very best that they can offer. In return they live from the Gospel. Even though the gospel is free, they still live from it. For them, when they preach - they can eat! (In this context what is free, is certainly not cheap!)

Consider this; we don't like parking our new cars just anywhere, do we? We prefer to put them where they'll be best-sheltered and taken care of. So why then should we be any less concerned or attentive when it comes to where we place our seed? It's not just a case of going through the motions and checking it off our to-do list. But it is a faith venture, that can bring awesome returns into our lives. Our aim is not to become like fat-cats living in the lap of luxury in terms of wealth - but that we can become more accessible to others, which can lead to a very fulfilling and rewarding life.

Aim and Fire!

Too many precious saints give without applying faith or with any revelation about what they are doing. Either that or the revelation they once had has become stale with misuse.

The effect of this is little if any reciprocation - which only feeds their unbelief, (that somehow giving just doesn't work for them!)

However proof is out there! There are innumerable testimonies that provide us with evidence that giving works, and always has. There is nothing warped or bias about God's system of doing things. We just have to do it HIS way. The Word works for those who work it. It takes more effort than just bucket plunking once a week; or simply allowing direct debits or standing orders to leave our accounts each month, (without being mindful of them). We must be more purposeful than that, in order to see the results of our giving. WE MUST AIM OUR FAITH LIKE A BOW AND ARROW! WITH GOD THERE ARE ALWAYS RESULTS.

Any lack of results, can be due to "giving-amiss" or "giving-lazily," without applying faith. It's time to check and assess ourselves and to stay where the blessings are! Because the more blessed we can be - the more richly positioned we can be in order to fulfil the destiny upon our lives while helping others to fulfil theirs. Having done all by faith - God is our greatest reward:

> *Without faith it is impossible to please him: for he that cometh to God must believe that he is, and that he is a rewarder of them that diligently seek him.*
>
> *(Hebrews 11:6 KJV)*

Reciprocal giving (giving with returns) should never stop us from "benevolence giving" (giving without return — such as alms deeds), because God will certainly have us engage in this kind of selfless-giving from time to time. For example, giving to the poor as the bible teaches, is equivalent to "lending to the Lord." And we can never out-give God. He is no man's debtor. **Alms deeds should be a fundamental part of our Christian life experience.**

❖

CHAPTER 10

Get in Line for a Spiritual Harvest!

We must **sow our precious seed into good soil and never sow under pressure.** God is faithful to speak to us and to direct us, thus enabling us to **give with joy.** Also we must avoid giving just random sums. Instead we must always ask God how much we are to give, because compulsive giving is emotionally driven, not faith or Holy Spirit inspired.

Other seed fell in rich earth and produced a bumper crop.
(Luke 8:4-15 MSG)

The devil does not want believers to be generous. If he can't stop our generosity, he'll seek to divert it, so that we contribute to the wrong things. If we sow into things that are not approved by God, the devil has managed to channel our money down a blind alley and prevented it from bearing fruit.

We should do nothing out of routine or religious duty, **but let it flow out as a result of our relationship with the Lord.** In this way, we will be actively involved in what God is doing.

Motives and Good Intentions

Similarly, we **should not allow threats or flattery to motivate our giving, as this is not the leading of the Holy Spirit** either. As soon as we feel under pressure to give, we must stop immediately. This is not the correct motivation for giving - and it's the "motivation" for giving that is the most critical issue. "If the willingness is there, the gift is acceptable according to what one has, not according to what one does not have" (2 Corinthians 8:12). God does not consider the amount of money given; **He looks at the motive behind the giving.**

Paul wanted to remind the believers in Corinth of their previous decision. Like the rest of us, they had a tendency to act on impulse and then go home and forget all about it. Now, a year later, Paul was writing to remind them of their decision. He said, "Now finish the work, so that your eager willingness to do it may be matched by your completion of it, according to your means" (2 Corinthians 8:10-12).

So here's what I think: The best thing you can do right now is to finish what you started last year and not let those good intentions grow stale, your heart's been in the right place all along. You've got what it takes to finish it up, so go to it. Once the commitment is clear, you do what you can, not what you can't. ***The heart regulates the hands…***

(MSG)

We must prove that we are willing to carry out our decisions. *God considers the promises that we make to be sacred and precious.* Just as His promises are precious to us, He wants the promises that we make to be equally precious, holy and reliable. (Most ministries that I know of, could wall paper their offices, with all the unfulfilled pledges they've received over the years!)

God is merciful. He fully understands our situation and will never condemn us. He sees our goodwill and intentions. But we should make sure that we do not forget what we have promised.

Releasing Seed by Faith not Coercion

There are two important sides to this issue: on the one hand, we must be sure to keep our promises and on the other hand, we must avoid getting into legalistic bondage, by letting others force us into making wrong decisions and doing things we would otherwise never do, [coercion: forcing people to act involuntarily].

God has established a financial plan for His Kingdom and it involves us **giving voluntarily** to His work. **This is a ministry to the Lord, which is no less holy than praise and worship.** One thing I regret over the years is a lack of sowing, where the future harvests could have been reaped from past seed. This of course was before I received revelation on **financial increase**.

The Church is caught up with how to get, more than anything else and mostly misunderstand the teaching that is given through great servants of God. Instead people use

God or the ways of God in order to furbish their own desires rather than the desires of His Kingdom. We must see that **true prosperity is more about giving than getting.** Having said that of course we need to reap the blessings to be able to give in the first place, but the harvest cannot come without the seed being planted. I believe that there are literally millions of people suffering right now because we are not giving, not as we should!

Also I can see that there are certain *categories* within the Church, some give and do not expect anything back. Others give but don't give into good soil (failing to be led by the Holy Spirit). Then there are those who give regularly and faithfully tithe; we can read testimonies where debts are being wiped off, salaries increased or substantial inheritances left behind. However this still seems to me to be the minority, rather than the majority!

Giving That's Inspired by the Holy Spirit

It's also important to state that God by the Holy Spirit will show you the fields to sow into and note: the **fields are always someone else's!** Yes you can sow into your own soil, obviously a farmer doesn't sow in someone else's field but into his own field but we still must remember that in the Kingdom of God, **a seed is something that we do for others that improves their welfare or increases them personally and makes their life easier.**

This can be done in a variety of ways. For example giving into certain ministries, who are helping others, can make your seed go further and reach more people. Ultimately our seed ministers and refreshes others, because giving is a ministry in itself.

Our harvests are the seeds of another's field; this is God's way of establishing. **You cannot establish unless you help someone else establish first!** You might say, like the world says, "Let me establish, have what I need first and then... perhaps, I will help someone else." The problem with this concept? That type of self-establishing never ends! "MORE, ME & I" are always first! Self and the flesh life are always greedy and needy. **But let me make it clear. God wants us to release our seed to invest in the harvest field.**

The results of all this will be twofold:

a) There will be a spiritual reaction: **salvation**

b) Prosperity will be manifest: **spiritual and natural wellbeing**

In other words, the Body of Christ will see growth in the establishing of the Church, with the finances to do the work of the ministry. And the people of God will be blessed in everything they do!

Let's look at Acts 2:42-47:

They devoted themselves to the apostles' teaching and to the fellowship, to the breaking of bread and to prayer. Everyone was filled with awe, and many wonders and miraculous signs were done by the apostles.

All the believers were together and had everything in common. Selling their possessions and goods, they gave to anyone as he had need. Every day they continued to meet together in the temple courts. They broke bread in their homes and ate together with glad and sincere hearts, praising God and enjoying the favor of all the people. And the Lord added to their number daily those who were being saved.

My belief is this, that if we take **KINGDOM MANAGEMENT FOR ANOINTED PROSPERITY** seriously this will not only bring a tremendous outpouring of the blessings of God but would also release the financial needs to the ministers of the gospel. **The end result would be revival!**

We pray for an outpouring, but perhaps God is waiting for us to pour out our wealth to **set in motion a sea of abundance** where blessings and miracles would be on the lips of every believer instead of just the few! Prosperity is not just for the minority, while everyone else is jealous; on the outside looking in No! If we operate the way God stipulates in His Word, there is more than enough to go around; it is His plan that everyone can prosper. This well known little motto is very true indeed: **"The Word works, for those who work it!"** (See Matthew 13:3-23; Mark 4:2-20)

CHAPTER 11

Victims or Investors?

I think that some folk imagine this "wealth of the sinners," to just drop into our laps! Okay the bible might say, **"...it is stored up for the righteous,"** however I am a great believer that it is **"as we work"** that God is able to promote us (with the best positions and wages to-boot!) But let's not forget that in most cases our finances come to us via employers who are not yet believers.

> *A good man leaves an inheritance [of moral stability and goodness] to his children's children, and the wealth of the sinner [finds its way eventually] into the hands of the righteous, for whom it was laid up.*
>
> *(Proverbs 13:22 AMP)*

This transaction of wealth from the wicked to the righteous takes place *as we work not just as we sit!* This is very similar to some believer's concepts of the rapture; we were never meant to be all and *"sedentary"* waiting for the rapture, rather we should be active and obedient until the very last moment (faith without works is dead).

However - dare it be said - concerning wealth some Christians should have released this wealth back into the Gospel via their tithes and offerings, but instead built themselves golden calves to worship!

Statistically there is enough money in the Body of Christ (even as we speak) to change the nations forever; but only 5% to 20% of the Body of Christ actively supports the Kingdom of God financially. How sad that is… things could be so different!

So as we pray for a mighty release of wealth - from the *"wicked"* to the *"righteous"* - that the Body of Christ might increase, let us also pray that any golden calves erected out of misguided *(mismanaged)* funds, be melted down and turned back into capital to be released into **furnishing the End Time Gospel Crusade to the Nations!**

> *But you shall [earnestly] remember the Lord your God, for* **it is He who gives you power to get wealth that He may establish His covenant which He swore to your fathers,** *as it is this day. And if you forget the Lord your God and walk after other gods and serve them and worship them, I testify against you this day that you shall surely perish. Like the nations, which the Lord makes to perish before you, so shall you perish, because you would not obey the voice of the Lord your God.*
>
> *(Deuteronomy 8:18-20 AMP)*

Stepping into God's System

When opportunities arise (and they do) to get angry over situations related to our finances, it is precisely then that we must remember the words of Jesus; "it is better to give than to receive..." because this truth will bring great liberty if it is willingly heeded to.

In all honesty, there are those times when the last thing any of us would do is **give!** But usually when we turn to the Lord and say, "Lord help! What would You do in this situation...?" GIVING is the first thing He requires of us! Giving gets us out of a knot and shuts the door on the devil! He can't move against it! He can't issue gossip against it either. Why? **The devil won't draw attention to honourable behaviour!**

Just for illustration sake, we had an opportunity recently to get all unsettled after being robbed financially by a certain reputable company. This company did us *"wrong"* in not too many words and our flesh wanted to rise up and get all carried away with itself. Emotions can run high in times like this and become extremely articulate! In fact at times like these anxiety, worry and fear like to waltz right in, and have a pity party - they need no introduction or invitation...!

But the Lord reminded us of a testimony that we had heard of; a Christian couple who had something very valuable stolen from them at a very inopportune time. They felt angry at first and upset but then the Lord broke into their thoughts and reminded them of a few things.

As a result, they decided to do something unusual; prayerfully before Him they chose to GIVE this valuable item to the thief! (The thief was unaware of this of course! However it was settled before the Lord, lifting the burden of un-forgiveness and opening up the way for blessing).

Victim to Investor

By doing this act of faith, this immediately changed their status from *"victim"* to *"investor!"* Their missing valuable item was no longer "stolen property" but a very generous "GIFT!" **Consider this: Satan can't steel anything from us that we have already given away!**

According to the bible in Proverbs 6:31, a thief found must *"restore sevenfold..."* what he has stolen, alternatively **a seed sown can get as much as a 100 fold in return!** (Mark 4:10) This alone reveals how much smarter it is to be a GIVER in life. So when we are tempted to play the role of victim, we must stay within the role of GIVER, it has a better rate of return!

100 times is considerably more than seven! So just for the sake of mathematics, we must consider the wiser option! Think about it, if we were robbed of something valuing £500 and only claimed back 7 times that value - we would have done better to have *given* it away (as a seed sown by faith) to claim up to 100 times the value in return! This is our scriptural right!

Look at it numerically - £500 x 7 is only £3,500 this is good but we can do better! Just by choosing to GIVE something and see it as a seed - we can then claim a 100x fold harvest and get £50,000 in return - what an awesome difference! See how it prospers us to do as Jesus said (Acts 20:35) "It is more **blessed** to give than to receive..." Hallelujah for the wisdom of God!

Another Opportunity to Prosper

And with just one step, we can go from anxiety, frustration and anger - to joy, relief, excitement, expectation and faith. And what was meant for harm, from the devil's point of view has now become an **"opportunity to prosper!"** God's system is not only higher but far better. Better for the outcome, better for the investment **and better for our health!**

Instead of losing sleep and losing out (getting angry and hurt), we can make a quality investment and gain every time! **This means we never lose... we can win every time!** If we respond by faith instead of fear!

God prospers us in more ways than one. There is more to this than finance alone. He prospers us in spirit, soul and in body. He prospers our minds for example with His wisdom, and increases our revelation and knowledge of His Word. In fact, everything that God touches eventually prospers, whatever realm it is in; spiritual, practical or mental.

As we "choose" to do things God's way we'll come out on top every time. (Head NOT the tail! This is God's plan for His children Deuteronomy 28:13). Choosing to bless — rather than curse. Choosing to give — rather than anger and un-forgiveness. Choosing to sow — rather than indignation. Choosing to invest — rather than holding on to something that's worthless.

God's ways always propel us from the "small and narrow" into the "large and wide" (Psalms 18:19; 31:8; 118:5). He removes us from the "petty" to the things of the "vast and great!" He widens the lens, He extends the prospects and He opens up the way. So let us overcome evil with good by taking up the opportunity to prosper rather than being robbed... investing rather than holding-onto... shutting the devil out rather than letting him in!

We can't Fail doing things God's Way!

Jesus said to bless our enemies. He was so wise when He said that, He knew exactly what for and for why! We look on His statement with such puny perspective sometimes — but Jesus knew the outcome of such behaviour... In fact when we look at things the right way around and respond correctly — whatever the devil lines up for our defeat, becomes our firm victory. **We can't fail doing things God's way!**

His unworried, unperplexed calmness and His "all-wise-plans" - supersede all else. So therefore finally let us dare to invest — bless our enemies and give rather than curse - only then can we **step back and let God step in! Let's see what He can do!**

❖

CHAPTER 12

Break Out Prosperity

The **English** word to **prosper** means to succeed, to flourish, to thrive and especially to have economic success. In **Hebrew**, the word most often translated *"prosperity"* or *"success"* is *tsaleach, pronounced "tsaw-lay'-akh," (#6743 in Strong's).*

The King James Version translates this word in 15 different ways, among which are: *come mightily, be profitable,* **break out***, be good, prosper,* **make prosperous***.*

The main idea of this verb is to: *accomplish, finish, complete and succeed.* Thus the primary meaning of *tsaleach* has to do with pushing forward; that is achieving some goal. There are several tenses of *tsaleach,* and they can be used to convey a variety of concepts.

I like the term **"break-out"** to refer to prosperity as **breaking out of the mould that life, culture and tradition puts on us.** We can jailbreak our circumstances. We can shake off the chains of the past and be free to move on. Prosperity is a real achievement. Jesus put poverty on the cross. Like a curse hung on a tree. Forever it can be conquered and overcome. I like to remind folk that the war has already been won, we just have a few battles to fight and even then we are only **"enforcing"** the victory won at the Calvary.

For this reason I declare the blood over everything, not out of ritual but revelation. Not unlike Benny Hinn and the late Derek Prince, I value the Lord's Supper very highly and would take it (in remembrance) every single day, if I weren't restricted by travel.

The Passover actually happened and is not just a tradition; it is very real to all those who apply it. Jesus still causes destruction to pass-over! Satan comes to steal, kill and destroy but Jesus remains our Passover Lamb! The finances of this kingdom should not influence the finances of God's Kingdom. We should prosper, regardless.

Helping Others to Prosper

When the world is in recession, we should still be **thriving!** In the opening paragraph of this chapter, you'll see that prosperity also means: **"to make prosperous."**

We should make the world sit up and look, "Hey what are those people doing?" Wherever we go, we possess that territory for the Kingdom of God. And when we move on, we move on, but until then it's going to look like Kingdom property!

This is how I run my personal life. Like Smith Wigglesworth, I own very few clothes. But what I do have, is smart and in order. I de-clutter regularly and keep everything neat. In fact my wife calls me a "neat freak" but I genuinely see the benefits. When others are encumbered by "stuff" I am free to move, to operate and to succeed because obstacles are not in my way. I stay on top of the weeds of life and keep the way clear so that when God says move, I can move without having to clear out the rubble first.

Even Nehemiah (2:11f) had to stop and clear the rubble away before progress could be made and there are times like that. But if in your personal life you keep things uncluttered and simple, it makes flowing with God a whole lot easier. Some people would love to serve God the way I have over the last thirty years or more. But "life" has gotten in their way. That's a shame because good intentions don't build for the Kingdom, only faith with-works can!

So yes let's be prosperous but also help "make" others prosperous (or at least feel the benefits of our prosperity!) Let it overflow and spill into their lives, so that they want the same. Everybody loves excellence. They might not admit it at first, but inevitably everyone is influenced by it. I have seen it so many times.

Prosperity is a Perception

The moral of the story is this: prosperity is not just about possessions and money. Prosperity is a perception. It's a way of thinking as much as anything else; where you refuse to think failure, only success. It's that basic half empty or half full concept. And wherever you go or whatever you have at the time: you do your best, behave your best and deliver your best and circumstances can't revoke that.

Nothing impedes your "thriving" mentality. It's neither a "striving" mentality nor a "surviving" mentality. Instead you feel and look and live as if you are "thriving" every single day of your life. No matter what is going on around you. You see the possibilities in everything and don't look for the problems — rather the solutions.

Now this is more than just positive thinking. Why? Because there is no denial in the existence of problems but instead of dwelling on them, you seek their solution. You are a fixer. Not a faultfinder or a problem finder, but a "solver!"

Taking on the Prosperous Attitude

Take on the prosperous attitude today. Like Brother Hagin often used to say about faith; **"If you believe something then act like you do, talk like you do and think like you do."** The same is true of prosperity, act like it, talk like it and think like it — regardless. **True prosperity is an attitude that affects your whole way of life,** not just your pocket book!

I have lived in some of the poorest areas, where folk depend so heavily on welfare, that you can read the day of the week by their emotions. It's so predictable; on payday everyone's mood is high but by the end of the week everyone is dark and depressed! They are up and down (bipolar) because their moods are dictated to by their bank balance or cash flow.

This is earthly and low level thinking. It keeps people down. **So I say we should "break out!"** Break out of the mould that has us locked down. Jesus said don't think about earthly things but what is above. Therefore it's vital we stay lifted, because it's so easy to be brought down by life. **We must keep our eyes lifted, our spirits lifted and our thoughts lifted to break out of the rut.**

True prosperity goes way beyond money and is a mentality that refuses to be put down by circumstance. It rises to the occasion — regardless. Perhaps it sounds just like faith, but **it takes real faith to live in true prosperity.**

❖

CHAPTER 13

The Spirit of Increase

In my travels recently God gave me a word, concerning the state of the Church and how He wants each one of us to receive strength and remain thirsty, so that we can be ready with our own **supply-of-the-Spirit**, to bring increase wherever we go!

Let's turn to 1 Kings 19:3-5:

*Then he was afraid and arose and went for his life and came to Beersheba of Judah [over eighty miles, and out of Jezebel's realm] and left his servant there. But he himself went a day's journey into the wilderness and came and sat down under a lone broom or juniper tree and asked that he might die. He said, **it is enough; now, O Lord, take away my life; for <u>I am no better than my fathers</u>**. As*

he lay asleep under the broom or juniper tree, behold, an
*angel touched him and said to him, **arise and eat**.*

(KJV)

When God Leaves us to Ourselves!

According to *Matthew Henry's Concise Commentary*
it was totally necessary for God to leave Elijah alone just
long enough, for him to arrive at the conclusion that in his
own human strength, he was "…no better than my fathers."
Only in God's ability can we truly be bold and courageous.
"Jezebel sent Elijah a threatening message. Carnal hearts
(such as Jezebel's) are hardened and enraged against God,
by that which should convince and conquer them. Great
faith is not always alike strong. He might be serviceable to
Israel at this time, and had all reason to depend upon God's
protection, while doing God's work; yet he flees.

His was not the deliberate desire of grace, as Paul's, to
depart and be with Christ. **God thus left Elijah to himself,
to show that when he was bold and strong, it was *in* the
Lord, and the power of His might; but of himself he was
no better than his fathers**. God knows what He designs us
for, though we do not, what services, what trials, and He will
take care that we are furnished with grace sufficient."

As depressed as Elijah might have been, and no matter
how earnest his plea to die, God preserved his life. Even had
an angel prepare his food!

And as he lay and slept under a juniper tree... Being
weary and fatigued with his journey... behold, then an
*angel touched him, and said unto him, arise, and eat; **so***

far was the Lord from granting his request to take away his life, that he made provision to preserve it; so careful was he of him, as to give an angel charge to get food ready for him, and then awake him to eat of it!

(Gill's Exposition of the Entire Bible)

God's strength is always made perfect in our weaknesses. Therefore it was vital for Elijah to recognise his own frailty once again. Who he was in his own strength! Only then did God move in to get Elijah back on his feet! **All the time God was Elijah's strength he could face anything and anyone.** But the minute he took his eyes off of God and allowed fear to overtake him, a single woman had him on the run for his life!

The Juniper Tree

The juniper tree was a shrub found in abundance in southern Palestine. It had long slender branches with small leaves and provided insufficient shade or protection from the sun! Representing man's failed attempts to remedy his predicament and provide inadequate solutions to his own pain.

In a similar way people tend to treat the local church like a juniper tree. They want a place of refuge, shelter and meeting with God. But it's actually meant to be a place of re-commissioning and hearing the voice of God, (a place of obedience) Matthew 28:19-20. NOT a place to dump-oneself-give-up-and-die! It's sad to say that many Christians are dead or inactive, even though they are in a **RESURRECTION** place!

*An angel touched him and said to him, <u>Arise and eat</u>. He looked, and behold, there was a <u>cake</u> baked on the coals, and a bottle of <u>water</u> at his head. And he **ate and drank** and lay down again. The angel of the Lord came the second time and touched him and said, <u>Arise and eat</u>, for the journey is too great for you. So he arose and **ate and drank**, and went in the strength of that food forty days and nights to Horeb, the mount of God.*

(1 Kings 19:5-8 AMP)

Five Steps that we Must Consider

Step 1. Elijah was told to "arise and eat." In verse 8 it says that he "ate and drank."

If we take this literally we can then say that Elijah was first instructed to eat, which corresponds to the Word of God. The Bread of Life that sustained and energised him, for a journey that was "too great" for him. **Life is too great for any of us, especially without the provision of God's Word in our lives.**

Many have the Logos Word of God. They know and can quote what the bible says, but they don't live it. Add to this fact that many can be part of a church and their lives are no different to those who aren't. Their struggles are just the same and there are no overcoming victories in their lives. What one really needs is the Rhema Word of God for every circumstance and situation. Only then can Christ stand in our midst and perform His Word in and through our lives.

Step 2. Elijah drank, representing none other than the Holy Spirit. Who can survive without life giving water? And who can function without the Spirit's operation in their lives?

Step 3. According to Ephesians 4:16 the word "increase" is directly linked to the word "supply." It speaks of the supply of the Spirit, that each member of the Body (Church) can make, through **"seeing, knowing and doing."** Increase comes as a direct result of each member making his or her supply of the Spirit. Contributing such things as time, talents, efforts, gifting and finances (Philippians 1:19).

*From whom the whole body fitly **joined together and compacted** by that which **every joint supplieth,** according to the effectual working in the measure of **every part, maketh increase** of the body unto the edifying of itself in love.*

(Ephesians 4:16 KJV)

The word *"supply"* in the Greek means: *"to furnish and to nourish."* **EACH MEMBER must contribute their supply of the Spirit *(that which God has specifically given them)*, if the Body is to increase and flourish in any way.** Therefore we must make our supply of the Spirit available, to the part of the Body that we are connected with.

Step 4. A supply of the Spirit is directly linked to prayer. In other words, prayer is always connected with a supply of the (Holy) Spirit.

*And when they had **prayed,** the place was shaken where they were assembled together; and they were **all filled*** *with the Holy Ghost, and they spake the word of God with boldness.*

(Acts 4:31 KJV)

*For I know that this shall turn to my salvation **through your prayer,** and the **supply of the Spirit** of Jesus Christ.*
(Philippians 1:19 KJV)

Step 5. How do we make our supply of the Spirit? By SEEING, KNOWING & DOING.

This is the ministry of the Holy Spirit and how He communicates with us and directs our lives. Only when we step out, (being responsive to what He's showing us) can the anointing and the power be released. We must therefore always seek to be responsive to the Spirit and stop being dignified-stuffed-shirts that do nothing (contributing no supply of the Spirit to the rest of the Body).

We must see what the Holy Spirit wants to do through us, then DO IT! **Only when each member brings his/her supply of the Spirit, can there be true INCREASE.**

❖

CHAPTER 14

True Partnership A Faith Venture

Paul had partners! They supported him in the ministry and with the spreading of the Gospel. They gave to him or his ministry-purpose on a regular basis, (although at times maybe not as regular as Paul would have liked!) Confirming this notion of **"regular commitment in giving"** is his writings in 1 Corinthians 16:2, where he says, "On the first day of the week let each one of you lay something aside..." (NKJ)

At the moment I have all I need – and more! I am generously supplied with the gifts you sent me with Epaphroditus. They are a sweet-smelling sacrifice that is acceptable and pleasing to God. And this same God who takes care of me will supply all your needs from his glorious riches, which have been given to us in Christ Jesus. Now all glory to God our Father forever and ever! Amen.

(Philippians 4:18-20 NLT)

Any ministry worth their salt will tell you that it's the regular income, that they can literally "bank" on, not just good-will gestures - no matter how nice they are! Many times have the earnest and regular giving of the few, provoked much praise from our lips!

God prospers us ultimately so that we can establish His Kingdom here on the earth, and "actively" seek first His Kingdom; in turn this brings a "supernatural flow" into our lives to meet all of our own needs (and let's face it, we are always going to have needs! So we must get this right; for the bigger picture and for our own!) Therefore as we pray for direction in our giving, and then couple it with corresponding action - we find that our own financial needs are taken care of, as promised in Matthew 6:33. Very few Christians truly understand the kind of partnership that Paul spoke of - systematic and deliberate giving - to benefit the Kingdom of God.

I have always believed that if I put God's house first then He will furnish mine! He has never failed me yet. **But my faithfulness in this transaction is the linchpin**. Without my corresponding action by faith, then I cannot tap the promises of God towards my own well being. Faith is dead without works or should I say that faith that is not working is dead! Acting in obedience brings results, for anybody.

It does not take a PHD or rocket science either, just faith working, faith moving; faith doing. This is the point behind giving. Not the amount given, rather the fact that your faith is mobilising itself and is the only thing that God can respond to - nothing else!

Think about it: if God responded to pain, need or lack, then there would be no poor places like India for example. But Jesus said we would have the poor with us "always." Not because God sanctions poverty, no! (the cross dealt with that fact). More to the point, is that Jesus knew His heavenly Father could only respond to faith and that not everyone would operate by faith, choosing the systems of this world instead. In that context, there will always be the poor amongst us.

God Responds to Faith

I repeat, God only responds to **faith.** And our giving must be done out of faith. In fact whatsoever is not of faith is SIN, (which is such a sober thought!) And we have all done things outside of the faith realm. But I have always believed, that those precious folk who have tithed faithfully for decades - yet never seen any financial freedom - contradict the very Word of God.

Why? Because it's not their giving that God responds to, it's their faith. Therefore no matter how admirable giving is, if it's not mixed with FAITH, how can He respond to it favourably? The ONLY thing that pleases God or provokes His favour is faith. It just stands to reason.

It also stands to reason that Satan works overtime to keep God's people ignorant about giving. And when Satan can't prevent saints from giving, he works to pervert their giving instead (to make it look like God's ways don't work and to promote unbelief). This is the very reason that pastors must keep their congregations well informed, about giving by faith and not emotional compulsions!

So having said all that, even our sincerity is no match for faith and lots of people are sincere but sincerely wrong! Therefore God does not even respond to our "sincerity," it's our faith alone that flicks His switch and nothing else (for want of a better term!) So with that settled, we shouldn't do anything without our faith backing it up; especially when it comes to giving. Because who wants to give into a black hole and not see a return? (Only pious religion looks for such punishment!)

Giving to Receive was First Instigated by God!

We must not forget that the whole **seed-time-and-harvest** scenario is a full on **give-and-receive-deal.** Think about it, even God gave Jesus expecting something in return (one son for many!) So we must not be deluded into giving without expecting. Because if we fall into the trap of giving without having faith attached, we will forever be unfruitful and disenchanted with the things of God. Tempted even, to turn and blame others (including God perhaps), for our barrenness, when in actual fact the responsibility for giving-by-faith, is ours alone!

Scripture is clear, *"Herein is my Father glorified that ye bear much fruit."* God never planned for us to be sterile or fruitless but utterly fruitful. Why? Because ultimately this is what glorifies Him.

It confuses folk, when we say we have a relationship with God and yet live like beggars. It doesn't fit right with them. They think, *"Is that how God treats His faithful ones?"* Needless to say it inspires no one to sign up! Who wants a faith that doesn't work? **Why would a turkey vote for Christmas?!**

On the contrary God wants our faith to work mightily and He wants others to **see it working,** this is our witness that if they too hook up with God, all things are possible. Otherwise it's just more of the same. Why believe in God at all? All unbelief is enhanced when the world watches powerless Christians for generations, blowing a lot of hot air without achieving very much! Yet what a reality check when they see true faith lived out!

So our giving, regardless of its amount or regularity, must be by faith. Regularity was even an issue with Paul. Think about it, when people only get behind the Good News worldwide mission once a year *(even if it's done by faith)* we are left on the mission field to struggle for the rest of the year, (Paul also knew how to abase and abound!)

However the mission of God cannot be reduced or limited by onetime or sporadic givers; compulsive or knee-jerk giving either! Think about it, God **never stops giving.** For instance His mercy is new **every day**. It's not a year old and wearing thin. No! Every single day He is giving to us. And it's that kind of constancy, that keeps us going over and not under.

This is also why ministries need faithful partners, who take hold of the vision constantly and not just periodically. Whose giving is not just an annual experience, to stop their conscience barking too loudly! As ministers we need those who will give as the Lord directs on a daily basis, weekly, monthly and annually. Those who keep their finger on the pulse, who care about the needs of the Kingdom and not just their own; these are the ones whom God is using to furnish this great end time revival. Others are much slower on the uptake!

Giving Makes Way for the Gift-bearer

Consider Proverbs 18:16 says, "A man's **gift maketh room for him,** and bringeth him before great men," understanding the true meaning behind this verse can change your life, because it's not talking about skills, talents or abilities but actual **gifts**.

The Hebrew word that was translated *"gift"* in Proverbs 18:16, 19:6, and 21:14 literally means *"present."* It's clear then that this scripture is NOT referring to the anointing or being highly favoured, but refers specifically to **"presents"** given.

Something spiritual happens when you simply give gifts, as the NIV puts it "...a gift <u>opens the way for the giver</u> and ushers him into the presence of the great." Notice that the emphasis is on the **giver** here and not the receiver; giving makes way for the gift-bearer not the recipient!

It's essential to understand, as Paul reiterates here in chapter 4 of Philippians, it's our giving that makes way for us: "Not that I desire your gifts; what I desire is that more be credited to your account... They are a fragrant offering, an acceptable sacrifice, pleasing to God" (v17-18). In other words, God seeks the result of the gift, more than the gift itself. "Not that I'm looking for handouts, but I do want you to experience the blessing that issues from generosity"

(MSG); "Not that I am looking for a gift—I am just looking toward your reward that comes from your gift" (VOICE).

**GOD IS NOT AFTER YOUR MONEY
BUT AFTER YOUR FAITH!**

❖

Bibliography

- Ekman, Ulf. The Church of the Living God. (101) Uppsala, Sweden: Published by Word of Life Publications. Copyright © 1994

- Ekman, Ulf. Financial Freedom. (113-114) Uppsala, Sweden: Published by Word of Life Publications. Copyright © 1989

- Jeffrey, Grant. Prince of Darkness. (105) Colorado Springs, Colorado USA: Published by WaterBrook Press. Copyright © 1994

- Munroe, Myles. Overcoming Crisis. (19, 20, 23, 39, 40, 44) Shippensburg, Pennsylvania USA: Published by Destiny Image. Copyright © 2009

- Prince, Derek. Orphans, Widows, the Poor and Oppressed. (17-19) Charlotte, North Carolina USA: Published by Derek Prince Ministries International. Copyright © 2000

- Strong, James. S.T.D., L.L.D. 1890. Strong's Exhaustive Concordance; Dictionaries of the Hebrew and Greek Words. e-Sword ® version 7.6.1 Copyright © 2000-2005. All Rights Reserved. Registered trade mark of Rick Meyers. Equipping Ministries Foundation. USA www.e-sword.net.

- Unless otherwise indicated, all scriptural quotations are from the HOLY BIBLE, NEW INTERNATIONAL VERSION ®. NIV ®. Copyright © 1973, 1978, 1984 by the International

❖

Ministry Profile

Doctor Alan Pateman, an apostle, is the President and Founder of **"Alan Pateman Ministries International"** (APMI), which was established in England back in 1987, a Christian-based *(parachurch)* non-profit and non-denominational outreach. This ministry is now focusing in two main areas: First **"Connecting for Excellence"** Apostolic Networking (CFE) and secondly, the teaching arm, **"LifeStyle International Christian University"** (LICU).

CFE is a multi-facetted missions organisation with the purpose of connecting leaders for divine opportunities and building lasting relationships, to touch the lives of leaders literally the world over. Apostle Dr Alan Pateman has to date ordained more than 500 ministers in over 50 NATIONS. In addition there are ministries, churches and schools who are in Association or Affiliation, looking to him for apostolic counsel and oversight.

Secondly LICU, which was founded in 2007, is a study program to help people discover their purpose and destiny. A global network of university campuses and correspondence students, demonstrating the Supernatural Kingdom of God through Doctrinal, Apostolic and Prophetic Teaching. Dr Alan holds the position of President/CEO, Professor of Theology, Biblical Studies and Apostolic Ministry. LICU is exploding throughout Europe, Asia and Africa, enhancing the Body of Christ

Dr Alan has authored more than 35 books including numerous teaching materials and LICU university courses (30) along with hundreds of Truth for the Journey articles on kingdom lifestyle *(that are regularly distributed globally via the internet).*

He is recognised as an Apostle, Bishop, Leadership Mentor, University Educator, Motivational Speaker, Connector and Author, who has also been featured on national and international TV and radio networks throughout the years.

Currently Apostle Alan, his wife Dr Jennifer reside in Lucca *(Tuscany)* Italy and travel out from their Apostolic Company.

- Alan Pateman Ph.D., D.Min., D.D., M.A., B.Th.

Academic Background

Dr. Alan Pateman attended several colleges throughout his training *(including studying Theology at Roffey Place, Horsham, UK and a Member of Kerygma - with Rev. Colin Urquhart and Dr. Bob Gordon - 1985-1987)* before being awarded a Doctorate of Divinity *(2006)* in recognition of his lifetime achievements by the International College of Excellence, now "DanEl Christian College" *(President: Dr. Robb Thompson USA)* also "Life Christian University" *(Dr. Douglas Wingate USA)* where he also earned a Bachelor of Theology B.Th. *(2006),* a Master of Arts in Theology M.A., a Doctor of Ministry in Theology D.Min., *(2007)* and Doctor of Philosophy in Theology Ph.D. *(2013)* from LICU.

❖

To Contact the Author

Please email:

Alan Pateman Ministries International

Email: apostledr@alanpateman.com
Web: www.AlanPatemanMinistries.com

*Please include your prayer requests
and comments when you write.*

❖

Other Books

Media, Spiritual Gateway

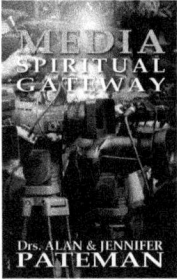

Let's face it; we live in the era of fake news! It's always existed, but never been quite so prominent. Today it's an all-out-war between fact and political fiction.

ISBN: 978-1-909132-54-2, Pages: 192, Format: Paperback, Published: 2018 *Also available in eBook format!*

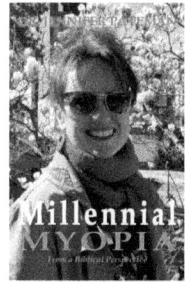

Millennial Myopia, From a Biblical Perspective

The standard for every generation is Jesus. However Millennial Myopia describes the trap of focusing everything on one particular generation or demographic cohort, at the exclusion and expense of all others. The Church cannot afford to make this mistake too.

ISBN: 978-1-909132-67-2, Pages: 216, Format: Paperback, Published: 2017 *Also available in eBook format!*

Truth for the Journey Books

TONGUES, Our Supernatural Prayer Language

In writing to the church at Corinth, Paul encouraged them to continue the practice of speaking with other tongues in their worship of God and in their prayer lives as a means of spiritual edification. "He that speaketh in an unknown tongue edifies, charges, builds himself up like a battery."

ISBN: 978-1-909132-44-3, Pages: 144,
Format: Paperback, Published: 2016
Also available in eBook format!

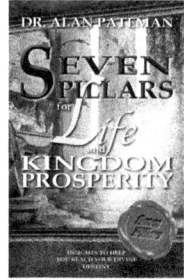

Seven Pillars for Life and Kingdom Prosperity

I submit these "Seven Pillars for Life and Kingdom Prosperity" to you, (Love, Prayer, Righteousness, Obedience, Connections, Management, Money). It's my desire that you walk in the triumphs that God has ordained for you.

ISBN: 978-1-909132-46-7, Pages: 220,
Format: Paperback, Published: 2016
Also available in eBook format!

Seduction & Control:
Infiltrating Society & the Church

This book is a glance into the world of seduction and control, how they try to influence the Church through many powerful avenues such as the New Age, sexual education in our schools, basic entertainment; things that touch our everyday lives in order that we effectively and gradually become desensitised.

ISBN: 978-1-909132-00-9, Pages: 156
Format: Paperback, Published: 2015
Also available in eBook format!

WINNING by Mastering your Mind

Someone once said, "Happiness begins between your ears and your mind is the drawing room for tomorrow's circumstances..." Remember, what happens in your mind will happen in time, and therefore one of our first priorities must be mind-management.

ISBN: 978-1-909132-40-5, Pages: 136,
Format: Paperback, Published: 2017
Also available in eBook format!

Why War: A Biblical Approach to the Armour of God and Spiritual Warfare

Spiritual warfare means different things to different people, but from a biblical standpoint Ephesians 6:10-18 gives us the best biblical definition of spiritual warfare possible. We can also see how God has thoroughly equipped us for victory not just self defence!

ISBN: 978-1-909132-39-9, Pages: 180,
Format: Paperback, Published: 2013
Also available in eBook format!

Forgiveness, The Key to Revival

Scripture is absolute when it comes to forgiveness. IF we forgive, THEN we are forgiven. It's that simple but no one said it was easy! Nonetheless, forgiveness can be likened to a spiritual key that unlocks spiritual doors and opportunities!

ISBN: 978-1-909132-41-2, Pages: 124,
Format: Paperback, Published: 2013
Also available in eBook format!

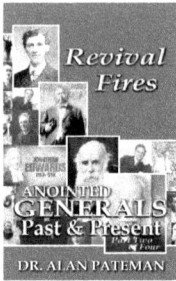

Revival Fires - Anointed Generals Past & Present (Part Two of Four)

Seasons might be changing but God's Word remains the same. The heart of the author is to help train, equip and be a blessing to those men and women who will be willing to fulfil their potential in ministry and be properly equipped for service.

ISBN: 978-1-909132-36-8, Pages: 142, Format: Paperback, Published: 2012
Also available in eBook format!

Prayer, Touching the Heart of God (Part Two)

Touching the Heart of God is the very essence of prayer. Whether we are petitioning God with very specific requests or consecrating ourselves before Him and rededicating our lives - whatever the case may be – the true essence of all praying is "Touching the Heart of God."

ISBN: 978-1-909132-12-2, Pages: 180, Format: Paperback, Published: 2012
Also available in eBook format!

Prayer, Ingredients for Successful Intercession (Part One)

This Book is the first of two books on Prayer. Dr. Pateman provides an exhaustive study, showcasing the vital ingredients necessary for all successful prayer. An excellent power-packed teaching tool, either for the individual or for the local church prayer group, that's eager to lay a solid foundation but don't know where to start!

ISBN: 978-1-909132-11-5, Pages: 140, Format: Paperback, Published: 2012
Also available in eBook format!

Apostles: Can the Church Survive Without Them?

Before Jesus returns a significant increase of the anointing will be poured out on the Body of Christ, but can the Church handle such an anointing? *(Acts 5:5)* Billy Brim once said, "As much as the anointing is powerful to create, it is as powerfully destructive of evil." The fear of God will be restored with the apostolic and people will begin walking with such anointing, as we have never seen before!

ISBN: 978-1-909132-04-7, Pages: 164,
Format: Paperback, Published: 2012
Also available in eBook format!

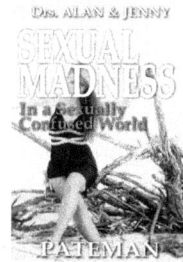

Sexual Madness: In a Sexually Confused World

This book discusses the sensitive subject of political correctness in our world today and the growing fear of causing offence in the public arena. It also discusses the rise of homosexuality, pedophilia and all other forms of sexuality, as there are many. Including modern statistics on pornography.

ISBN: 978-1-909132-02-3, Pages: 160,
Format: Paperback, Published: 2012
Also available in eBook format!

His Life is in the Blood

Blood is the trophy of every battle. The spilt blood of Jesus Christ is our trophy. It is our freedom from sin and bondage. Nothing can enter the blood-bought temples of the Holy Ghost! This book will encourage you to apply the blood of Jesus our Passover Lamb to your life, just as the children of Israel did in the Old Testament. Not merely talking or reading about it, but applying it.

ISBN: 978-1-909132-06-1, Pages: 152,
Format: Paperback, First Published: 2007
Also available in eBook format!

LIFESTYLE UNIVERSITY

Raising Up
Christian Leaders

Dear Friends,

Have you considered becoming one of our international students? We are privileged to welcome you, from around the world, to "LifeStyle International Christian University" *(the teaching arm of Alan Pateman Ministries International).* **An English speaking university** dedicated to your success; to see you trained and equipped to fully succeed in your God given Destiny.

It is our passion to raise up the leaders of tomorrow, who will have influence in all realms of authority, including the Body of Christ. Men and women of strategy, wisdom and true godliness, who'll stand with stature and maturity in this hour.

It's undeniable that in today's world, recognised education has become indispensable, therefore it is our desire to offer well balanced and well structured courses. Those that have been written by gifted and talented ministers of God, who seek to be inspired by God's Holy Spirit.

Consequently we have put together a **flexible curriculum,** designed both for correspondence students and campuses, which is a strategy to reach the distant learner; whether provincial, national or international. In fact we have many correspondence students from around the world, including a growing number of successful campuses, in various countries.

This is a growing platform, where men and women of dignity and passion, can grow and be established in their God given endeavours. As God is the healer of the nations, we pray and believe that many of our alumni will go on to **become world changers** in their own right.

We are proud of each and every one of our LICU students.
It would be our pleasure if you would join them on this incredible journey!

Doctor Alan Pateman

Alan Pateman Prof. Ph.D., D.Min., D.D., M.A., B.Th.
PRESIDENT AND CEO
www.licuuniversity.com   www.cfeapostolicnetwork.com
Email: info@licuuniversity.com   Mob: +39 366 329 1315

For more information visit our website/facebook or contact our office, using the details below:

Website: www.licuuniversity.com
Facebook: www.facebook.com/LICUMainCampus
Email: info@licuuniversity.com
Telephone: +39 366 329 1315

All Books Available

at

APMI PUBLICATIONS

Email: publications@alanpateman.com
*Also Available from Amazon.com
and other retail outlets.*

*If you purchased this book through Amazon.com
or other and enjoyed reading it, or perhaps one of
my other books, I would be grateful if you could
take a couple of minutes to write a Customer
Review, many thanks.*

www.ingramcontent.com/pod-product-compliance
Lightning Source LLC
Chambersburg PA
CBHW060041210326
41520CB00009B/1226